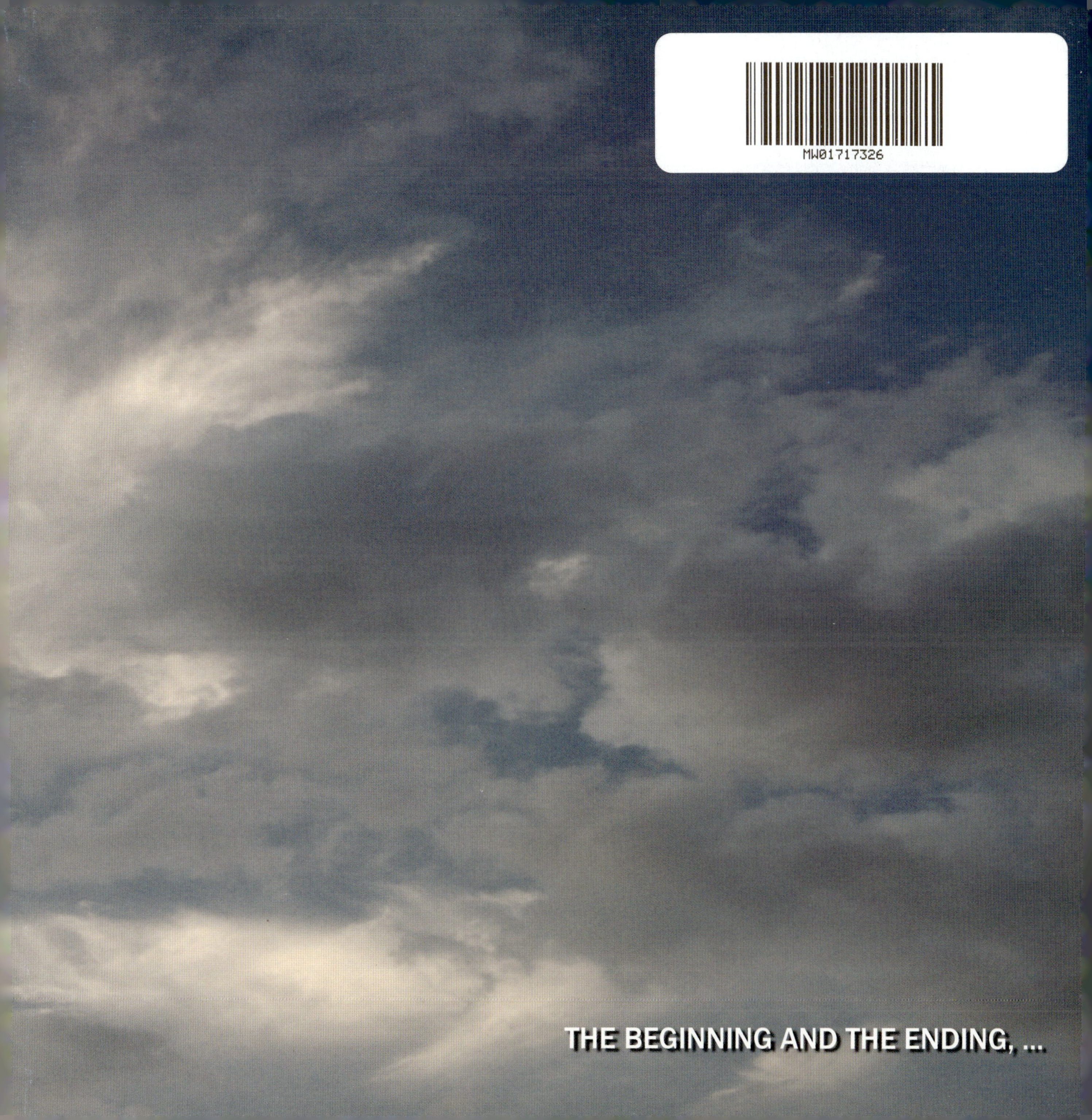
THE BEGINNING AND THE ENDING, ...

Tabernacle for a Shadow

Susan L. Conner

Waterworks Publishing
Naples, FL 34108

Tabernacle for a Shadow

Glory to God!

Published by
Waterworks Publishing
792 100th Ave. N., Naples, FL 34108
239-597-6398

All Scripture verses are taken from the King James Version of the Bible

Printed and bound in Hong Kong

Library of Congress Cataloging-in-Publication Data

Library of Congress Control Number: 2008926505

Conner, Susan L.
Tabernacle for a shadow / Susan L. Conner

Includes bibliographical references and index.

ISBN 978-0-9662520-8-8

14 13 12 11 10 09 08
7 6 5 4 3 2 1

In the name of the

Lord Jesus **THANK YOU** God and Father

for the inspiration and dedication to complete this book.

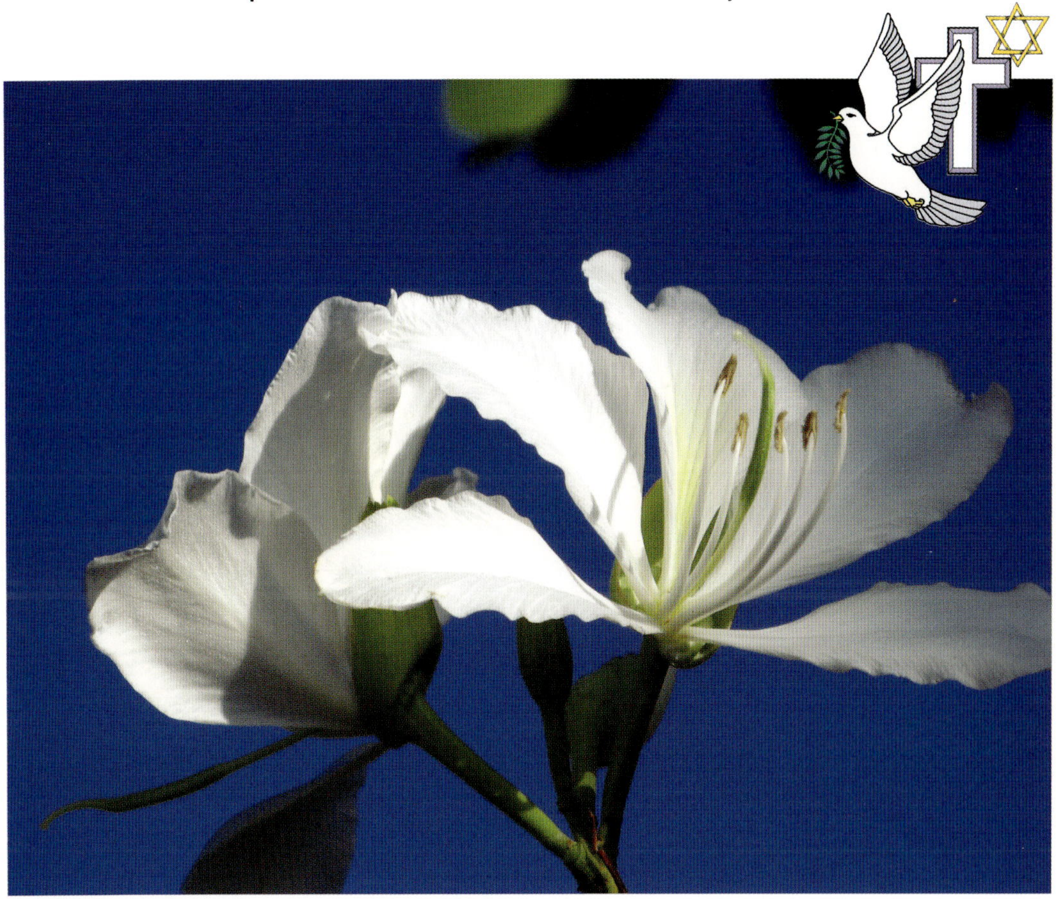

And whatsoever ye do in word or deed,
do all in the name of the Lord Jesus,
giving thanks to God and the Father by him.
Colossians 3 : 17

Dear Father and God, in the name of our Lord Jesus,

When You came to take my beloved Lloyd home to be with You,
You opened a whole new understanding of heaven and my purpose here.
What a gift!
Losing him was difficult and painful,
but You comforted me and gave me meaningful and joyous work.
When You led me to the beach that morning and let me view through Your eyes
what would become the cover of this book, I was amazed.
When You revealed to me the verse that would become the title of this book, I was shocked.
So began my powerful journey into a deeper understanding of You through Your Word.

When You revealed Your purpose to use one photograph with each book of the Bible,
little did I know that You would use my 25 year passion of taking photos in nature.
But You knew.

Limited by my ability to travel, all pictures are within the borders of the United States.
But God, You are not limited to where You will take this book.
You have revealed to me that You want it to a be a teaching tool for the lost,
as well as a devotional for the believers and a blessing for all Your children.

Thank you for establishing my thoughts, my words, and my steps.
I dedicate this book and all my work to You.
May it be pleasing to You and used for Your Glory.

You have healed this broken vessel in the process;
and it is my hope that this book will help others to be closer to You.
Thank you for allowing me to share my love for You and Your Word.

You are truly an Awesome God!

All my love,
Susan Lynn Conner

Thank You Jesus for sending two loving men into my life.

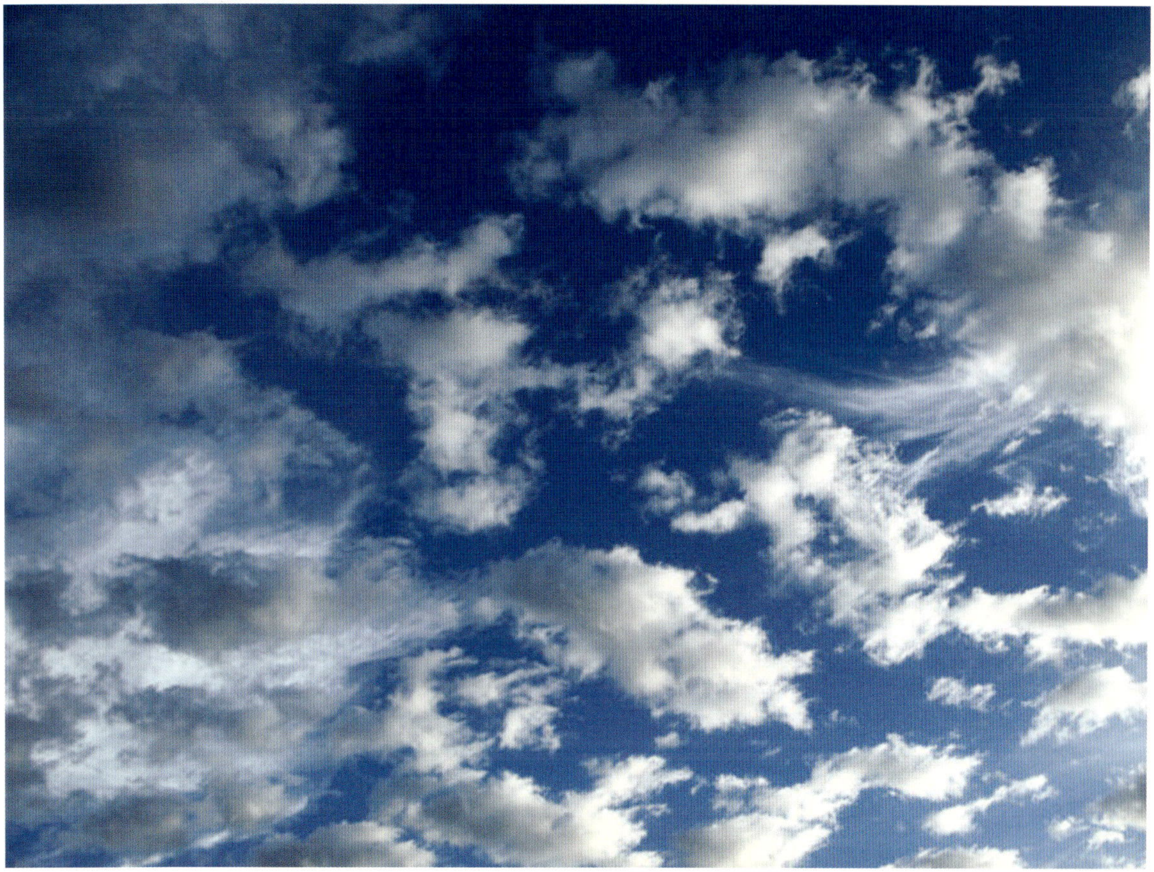

Thank you for the assurance that their souls are in heaven with You where I will one day be, too.

In loving memory of:

Murray A. Boutilier
9/24/21 - 12/19/06
my dad,
who loved his family even though
he did not come to know You personally
until near his death at age 85.

Lloyd A. Freeman
10/24/48 - 3/8/05
my sweetheart,
Your servant from the age of 12
who's love for You so overflowed onto me
that it carries on into eternity ...

For he that is called in the Lord, *being* a servant, is the Lord's freeman;
likewise also he that is called, *being* free, is Christ's servant.
1 Corinthians 7 : 22

To The Reader,

I am thankful to be the chosen vessel through which the Lord has poured out His Holy Spirit in the form of this photographic book of a sampling of His Word. It is meant to be an example of God's love revealed to us through His creation.

Moses was admonished to
"...see that you make all things according to the pattern showed you..." (Hebrews 8:5).
Much like he did, I have followed God's directions to the best of my ability.
God's instructions to me did not include any commentary on His Word other than this brief note to help the reader understand my purpose.

The King James Version of the Bible was chosen by God for me to use.
If there are words, phrases or concepts in this book that you do not understand,
I urge you to use some of the many resources available to enhance your study of the Word.

Some words used in the King James Version may seem obsolete, be spelled differently, or we may interpret them differently today than in the time when the words were written.
For example, in Song of Solomon 2:12 (page 43), it says "and the sound of the turtle... ,"
you might think, what sound does a turtle make?
If you looked up the word "turtle" in a Bible concordance,
you would see that what is referred to here is a turtle<u>dove</u>.

Capitalized words or sentences in both Old and New Testaments are to show that GOD is speaking as the Father, the Son, or the Holy Spirit.
LORD is capitalized in the Old Testament, refering to YHWH, the name of the God of Israel.
Italicized words are added by the translators of the King James Bible to help the reader to understand the meaning of some sentences.
The King James Bible does not capitalize personal pronouns when referring to God, so I have not capitalized them either except in my personal letter to God and this note to you.

The Lord wants us to seek Him. Study His Word. Find His Truth.
Do not allow the enemy to deceive you or hinder you in your search for God's wisdom.
I pray that God will inspire you and show new revelations to you as you read this book.

Thank you. I hope you enjoy the journey and may God abundantly bless you!

ACKNOWLEDGEMENTS

A Heartfelt Thank You!

*The list of names of those I wish to thank would take another book, so
I pray that you will find yourself among these:*

*To my mom and brother
and all of my dear family and friends, including my church family,
who prayed, prophesied, proof-read, promoted, printed,
encouraged, donated, supported and sacrificed
both with time and finances to help in the completion of this book.*

*To all the saints in Christ Jesus and those of the Jewish faith who have gone before me
and paved the way for this book to have it's place in God's time.*

To all those who saw the vision with me for the glory this book would bring to God.

*To all those who had enough faith to purchase this book before it's completion,
knowing that I would be faithful to God to complete the work He had started in me.*

*To all those who unselfishly purchased or will purchase this book for others
foreseeing the joy that it will bring to their loved ones.*

To all those who will find a new awareness of God's love through this book.

To all those who will use this book as a tool to teach others of God's eternal love.

In every thing give thanks:
for this is the will of God in Christ Jesus concerning you.
1 Thessalonians 5 : 18

OLD TESTAMENT

Pages	Book	Verses
1 - 2	Genesis	1 : 1 - 4
3 - 4	Exodus	17 : 3 - 6
5 - 6	Leviticus	23 : 40 - 43
7 - 8	Numbers	9 : 15 - 18
9 - 10	Deuteronomy	32 : 1 - 4
11 - 12	Joshua	24 : 2 - 4
13 - 14	Judges	7 : 2 - 4
15 - 16	Ruth	1 : 15 - 17
17 - 18	1 Samuel	17 : 39 - 40, 47, 50
19 - 20	2 Samuel	23 : 1 - 5
21 - 22	1 Kings	14 : 15 - 16
23 - 24	2 Kings	2 : 11 - 13
25 - 26	1 Chronicles	16 : 23 - 32
27 - 28	2 Chronicles	25 : 18 - 20
29 - 30	Ezra	8 : 21 - 23
31 - 32	Nehemiah	9 : 26 - 27
33 - 34	Esther	7 : 4 - 8
35 - 36	Job	19 : 7 - 8 & 23 - 27

TABLE OF CONTENTS

Pages	Book	Verses
37 - 38	Psalms	103 : 15 - 19
39 - 40	Proverbs	3 : 1 - 8
41 - 42	Ecclesiastes	3 : 1 - 11
43 - 44	Song of Solomon	2 : 10 - 13
45 - 46	Isaiah	1 : 15 - 18
47 - 48	Jeremiah	12 : 10 - 12
49 - 50	Lamentations	5 : 15 - 22
51 - 52	Ezekiel	36 : 26 - 30
53 - 54	Daniel	2 : 19 - 23
55 - 56	Hosea	14 : 4 - 8
57 - 58	Joel	2 : 25 - 29
59 - 60	Amos	5 : 20 - 27
61 - 62	Obadiah	1 : 16 - 19
63 - 64	Jonah	1 : 17 - 2 : 1 - 7
65 - 66	Micah	7 : 18 - 20
67 - 68	Nahum	1 : 1 - 4
69 - 70	Habakkuk	2 : 1 - 4
71 - 72	Zephaniah	1 : 2 - 6
73 - 74	Haggai	1 : 11 - 13
75 - 76	Zechariah	3 : 6 - 10
77 - 78	Malachi	1 : 11 - 13

Genesis 1 : 1-4

In the beginning God created the heaven and the earth.

And the earth was without form,
and void;
and darkness *was* upon the face of the deep.
And the Spirit of God moved upon the face of the waters.

And God said,
LET THERE BE LIGHT:
and there was light.

And God saw the light,
that *it was* good:
and God divided the light from the darkness.

and God divided the light

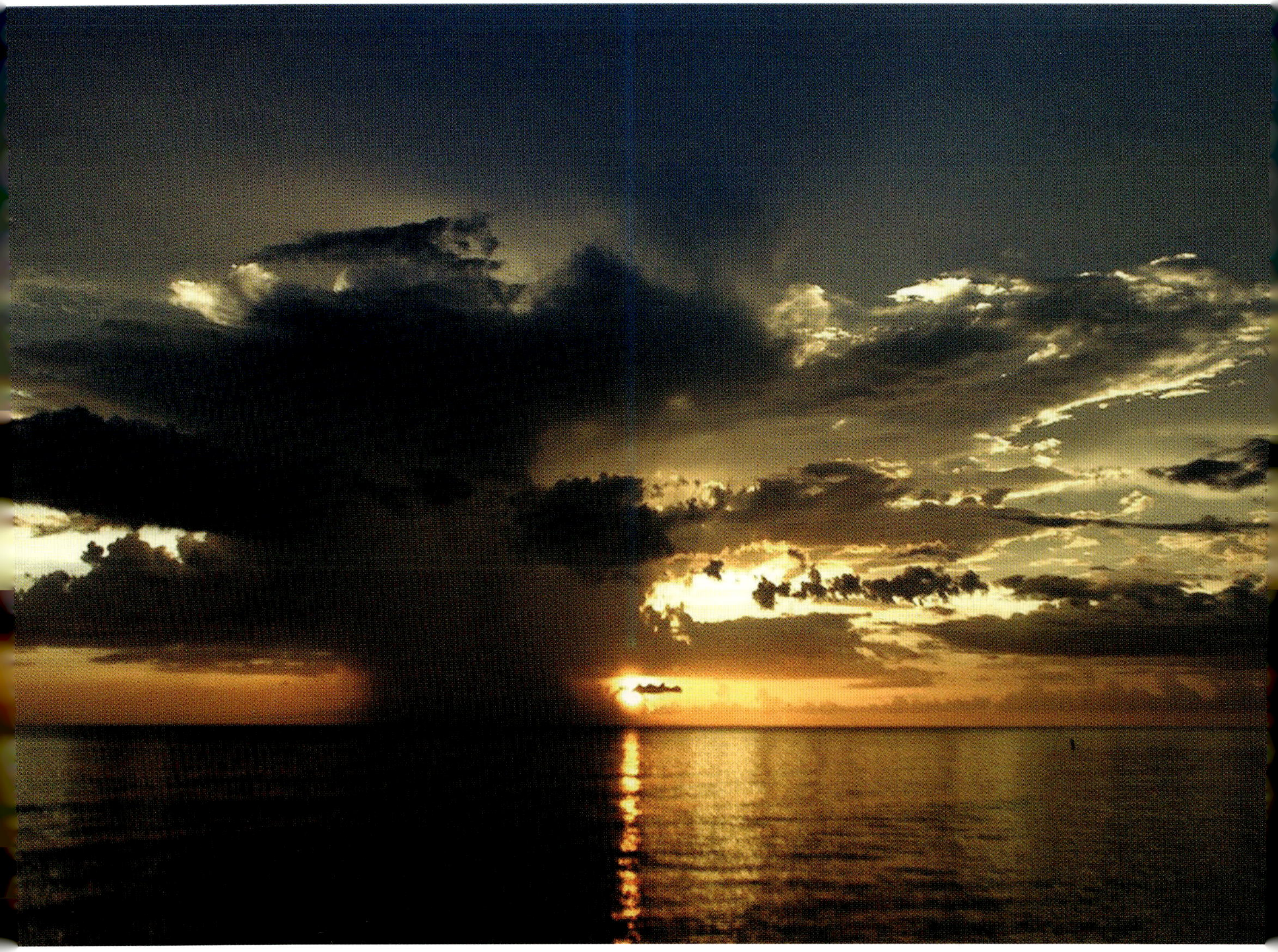

from the darkness

Exodus 17 : 3-6

And the people thirsted there for water;
and the people murmured against Moses,
and said,
Wherefore *is* this *that* thou hast brought us up out of Egypt,
to kill us and our children and our cattle with thirst?

And Moses cried unto the LORD,
saying,
What shall I do unto this people?
they be almost ready to stone me.

And the LORD said unto Moses,
GO ON BEFORE THE PEOPLE,
AND TAKE WITH THEE OF THE ELDERS OF ISRAEL;
AND THY ROD, WHEREWITH THOU SMOTEST THE RIVER,
TAKE IN THINE HAND, AND GO.

BEHOLD,
I WILL STAND BEFORE THEE THERE UPON THE ROCK IN HOREB;
AND THOU SHALT SMITE THE ROCK,
AND THERE SHALL COME WATER OUT OF IT,
THAT THE PEOPLE MAY DRINK.
And Moses did so in the sight of the elders of Israel.

AND
THOU
SHALT
SMITE
THE
ROCK,

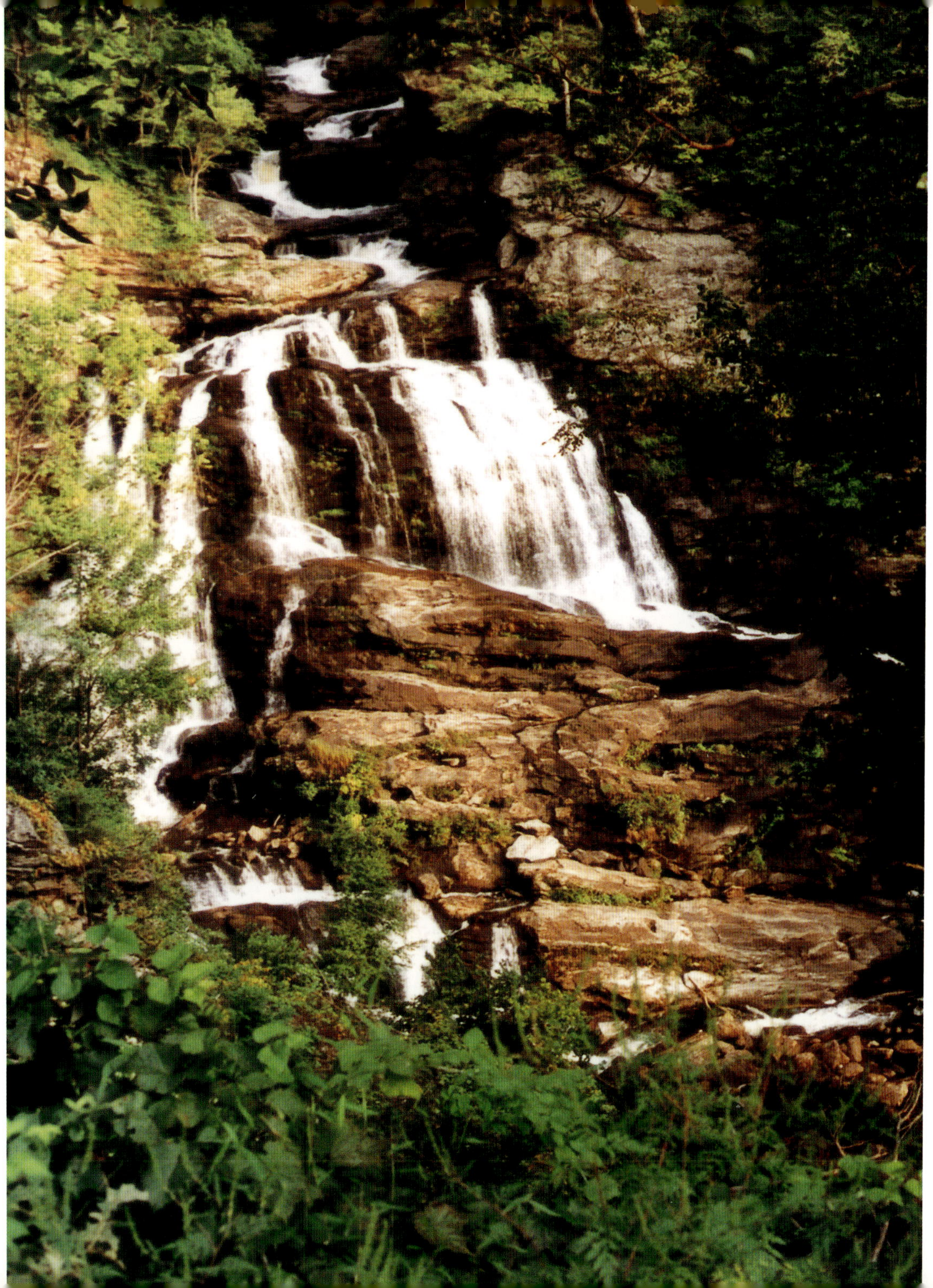

AND
THERE
SHALL
COME
WATER
OUT
OF IT

Leviticus 23 : 40-43

AND YE SHALL TAKE YOU ON THE FIRST DAY
THE BOUGHS OF GOODLY TREES,
BRANCHES OF PALM TREES,
AND THE BOUGHS OF THICK TREES,
AND WILLOWS OF THE BROOK;
AND YE SHALL REJOICE BEFORE THE LORD YOUR GOD SEVEN DAYS.

AND YE SHALL KEEP IT A FEAST UNTO THE LORD SEVEN DAYS IN THE YEAR.
IT SHALL BE A STATUTE FOR EVER IN YOUR GENERATIONS;
YE SHALL CELEBRATE IT IN THE SEVENTH MONTH.

YE SHALL DWELL IN BOOTHS SEVEN DAYS;
ALL THAT ARE ISRAELITES BORN SHALL DWELL IN BOOTHS:

THAT YOUR GENERATIONS MAY KNOW
THAT I MADE THE CHILDREN OF ISRAEL TO DWELL IN BOOTHS,
WHEN I BROUGHT THEM OUT OF THE LAND OF EGYPT:
I *AM* THE LORD YOUR GOD.

THE BOUGHS OF GOODLY TREES,

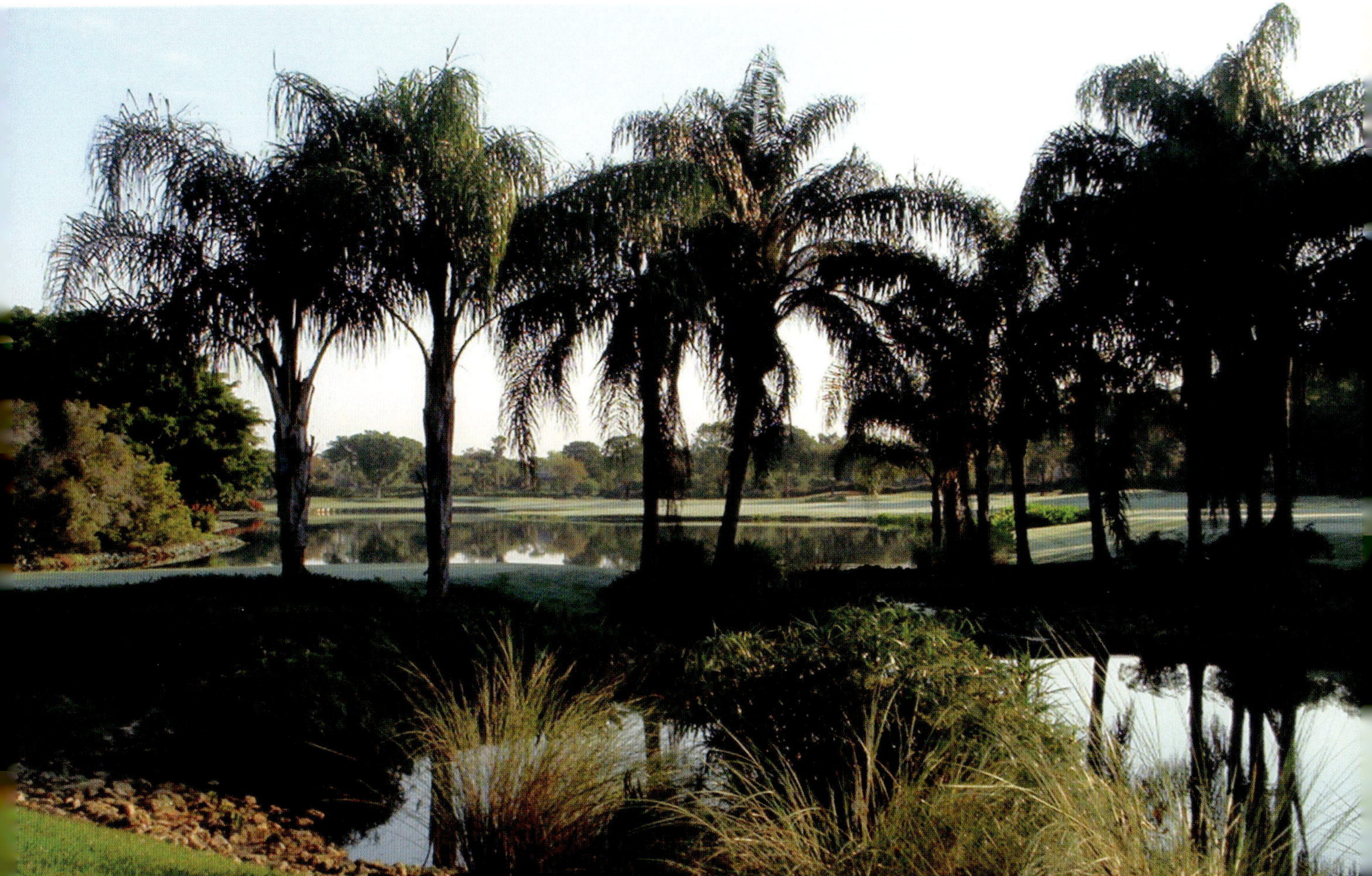

BRANCHES OF PALM TREES

Numbers 9 : 15-18

And on the day that the tabernacle was reared up
the cloud covered the tabernacle,
namely, the tent of the testimony:
and at even there was upon the tabernacle
as it were the appearance of fire,
until the morning.

So it was alway: the cloud covered it *by day,*
and the appearance of fire by night.

And when the cloud was taken up from the tabernacle,
then after that the children of Israel journeyed:
and in the place where the cloud abode,
there the children of Israel pitched their tents.

At the commandment of the LORD the children of Israel journeyed,
and at the commandment of the LORD they pitched:
as long as the cloud abode upon the tabernacle they rested in their tents.

the cloud covered it *by day,*

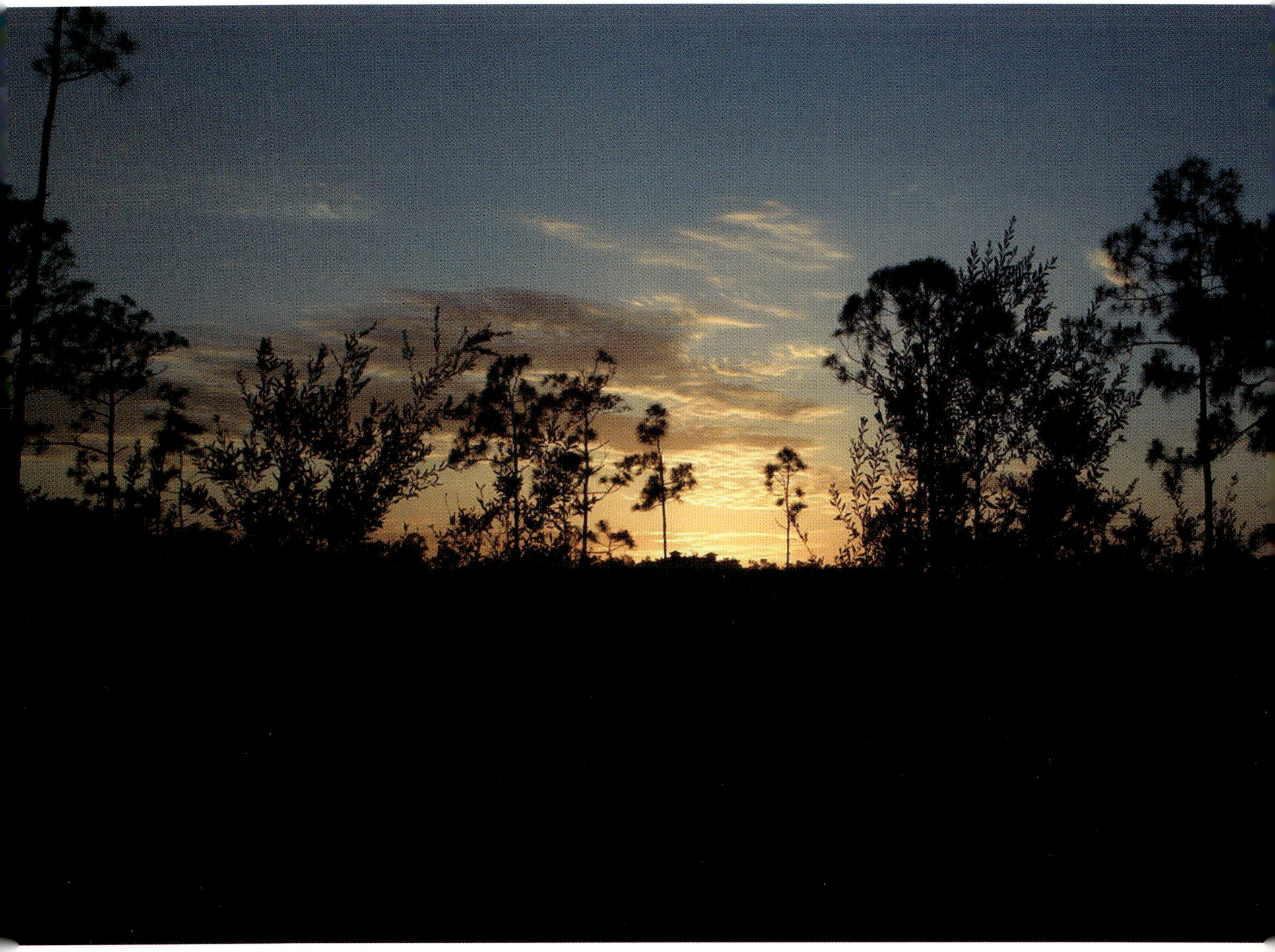

and the appearance of fire by night

Deuteronomy 32 : 1-4

Give ear,
O ye heavens,
and I will speak;
and hear,
O earth,
the words of my mouth.

My doctrine shall drop as the rain,
my speech shall distil as the dew,
as the small rain upon the tender herb,
and as the showers upon the grass:

Because I will publish the name of the LORD:
ascribe ye greatness unto our God.

He is the Rock,
his work *is* perfect:
for all his ways *are* judgement:
a God of truth and without iniquity,
just and right *is* he.

My doctrine shall drop as the rain,

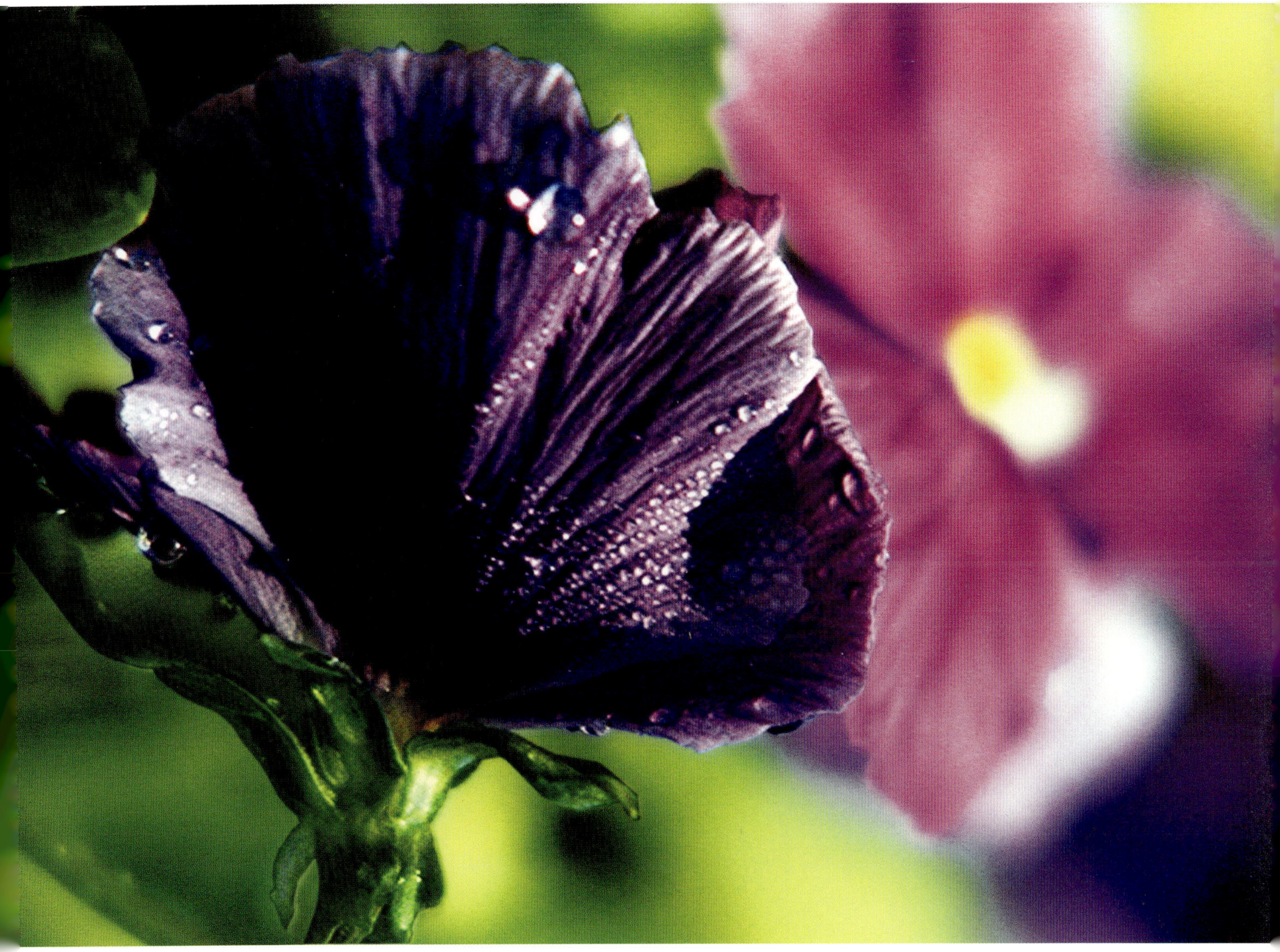

my speech shall distil as the dew

Joshua 24 : 2-4

And Joshua said unto all the people,
Thus saith the LORD God of Israel,
YOUR FATHERS DWELT ON THE OTHER SIDE
OF THE FLOOD IN OLD TIME,
EVEN TERAH,
THE FATHER OF ABRAHAM,
AND THE FATHER OF NACHOR:
AND THEY SERVED OTHER GODS.

AND I TOOK YOUR FATHER ABRAHAM
FROM THE OTHER SIDE OF THE FLOOD,
AND LED HIM THROUGHOUT ALL THE LAND OF CANAAN,
AND MULTIPLIED HIS SEED,
AND GAVE HIM ISAAC.

AND I GAVE UNTO ISAAC JACOB AND ESAU:
AND I GAVE UNTO ESAU MOUNT SEIR,
TO POSSESS IT;
BUT JACOB AND HIS CHILDREN WENT DOWN INTO EGYPT.

AND I TOOK YOUR FATHER ABRAHAM

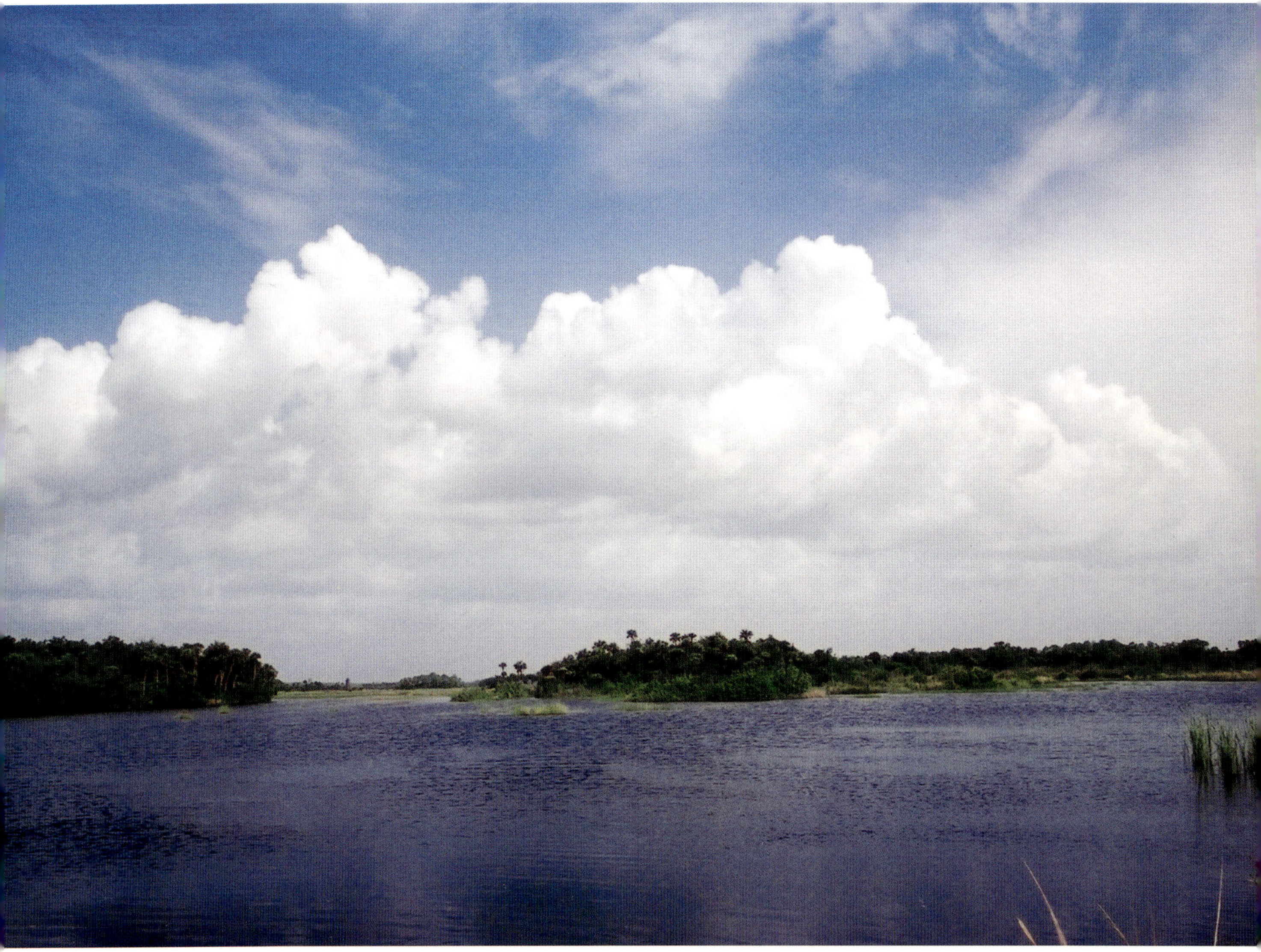

FROM THE OTHER SIDE OF THE FLOOD

Judges 7 : 2-4

And the LORD said unto Gideon,
THE PEOPLE THAT *ARE* WITH THEE *ARE* TOO MANY
FOR ME TO GIVE THE MIDIANITES INTO THEIR HANDS,
LEST ISRAEL VAUNT THEMSELVES AGAINST ME,
SAYING, MINE OWN HAND HATH SAVED ME.

NOW THEREFORE GO TO,
PROCLAIM IN THE EARS OF THE PEOPLE, SAYING,
WHOSOEVER *IS* FEARFUL AND AFRAID,
LET HIM RETURN AND DEPART EARLY FROM MOUNT GILEAD.
And there returned of the people twenty and two thousand;
and there remained ten thousand.

And the LORD said unto Gideon,
THE PEOPLE *ARE* YET *TOO* MANY;
BRING THEM DOWN UNTO THE WATER,
AND I WILL TRY THEM FOR THEE THERE:
AND IT SHALL BE, *THAT* OF WHOM I SAY UNTO THEE,
THIS SHALL GO WITH THEE,
THE SAME SHALL GO WITH THEE;
AND OF WHOMSOEVER I SAY UNTO THEE,
THIS SHALL NOT GO WITH THEE,
THE SAME SHALL NOT GO.

BRING
THEM
DOWN
UNTO

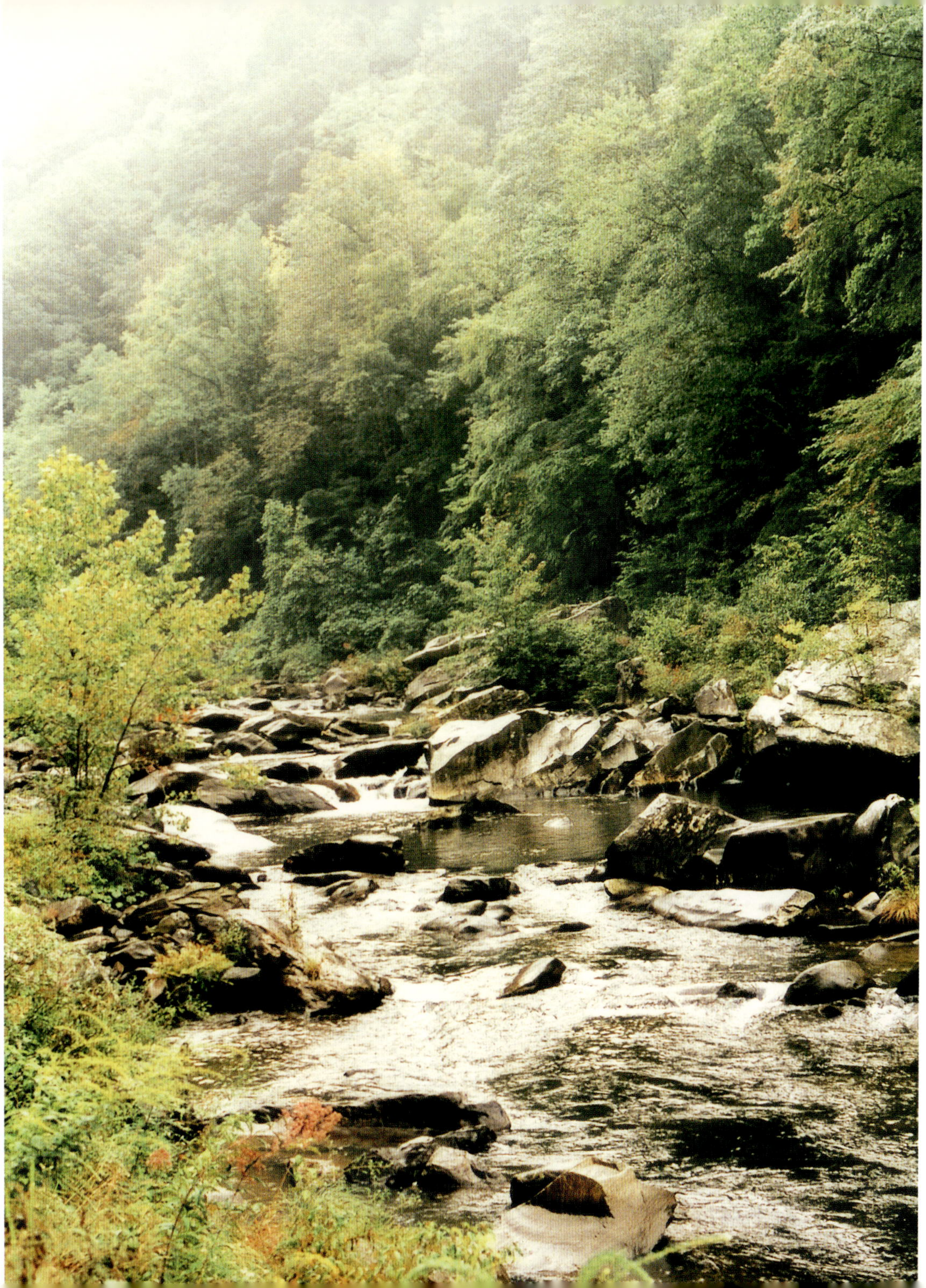

THE
WATER

Ruth 1 : 15-17

And she said,
Behold, thy sister in law is gone back unto her people,
and unto her gods:
return thou after thy sister in law.

And Ruth said,
Intreat me not to leave thee,
or to return from following after thee:
for whither thou goest,
I will go;
and where thou lodgest,
I will lodge:
thy people *shall be* my people,
and thy God my God:

Where thou diest,
will I die,
and there will I be buried:
the LORD do so to me,
and more also,
if ought but death part thee and me.

For whither thou goest,

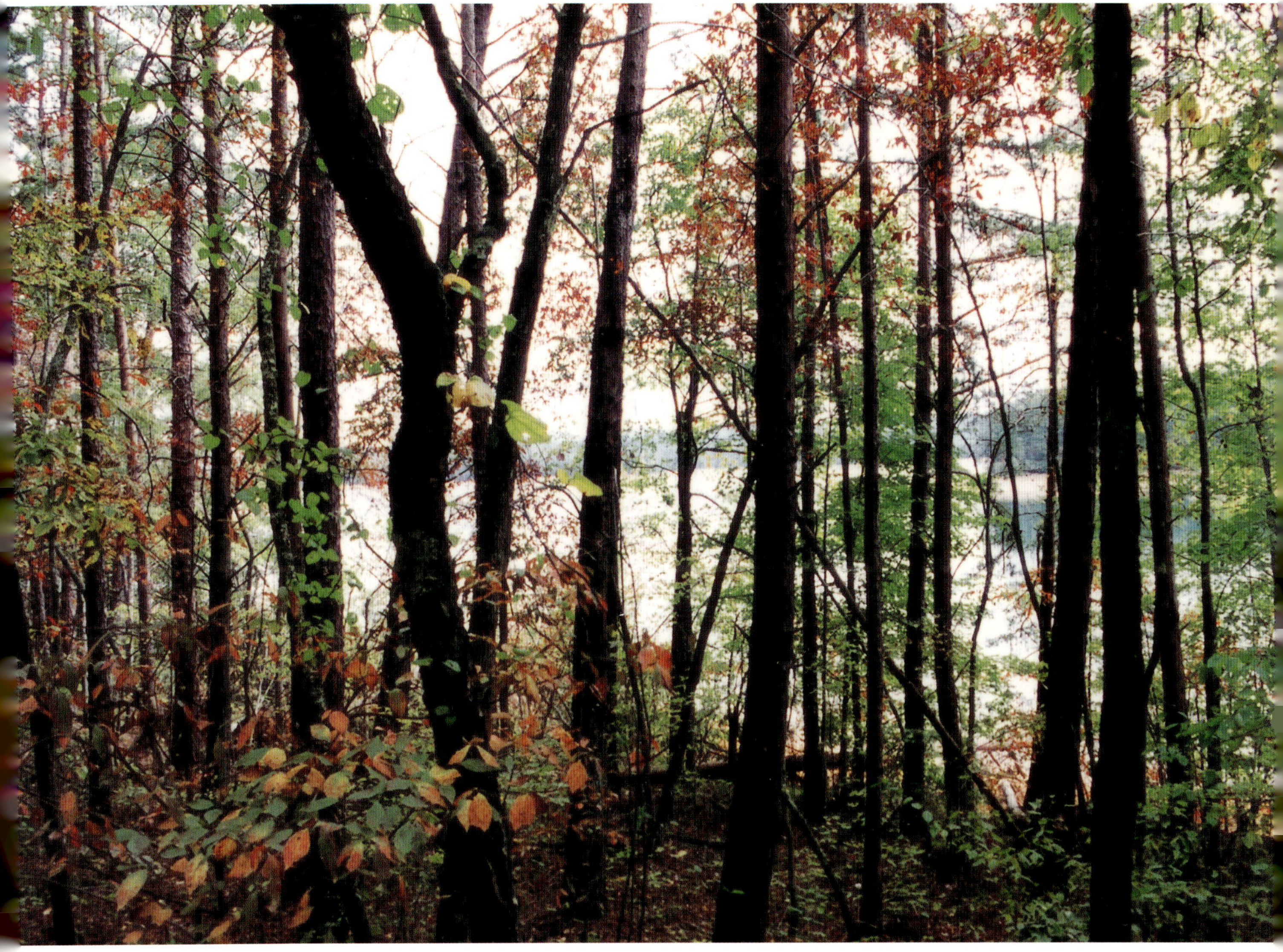

I will go

1 Samuel 17 : 39-40

And David girded his sword upon his armour,
and he assayed to go; for he had not proved *it*.
And David said unto Saul,
I cannot go with these; for I have not proved *them.*
And David put them off him.

And he took his staff in his hand,
and chose him five smooth stones out of the brook,
and put them in a shepherd's bag which he had, even in a scrip;
and his sling *was* in his hand: and he drew near to the Philistine.

1 Samuel 17 : 47

And all this assembly shall know that the LORD saveth not with sword and spear:
for the battle *is* the LORD'S, and he will give you into our hands.

1 Samuel 17 : 50

So David prevailed over the Philistine with a sling and with a stone,
and smote the Philistine, and slew him;
but *there was* no sword in the hand of David.

and chose him five smooth stones

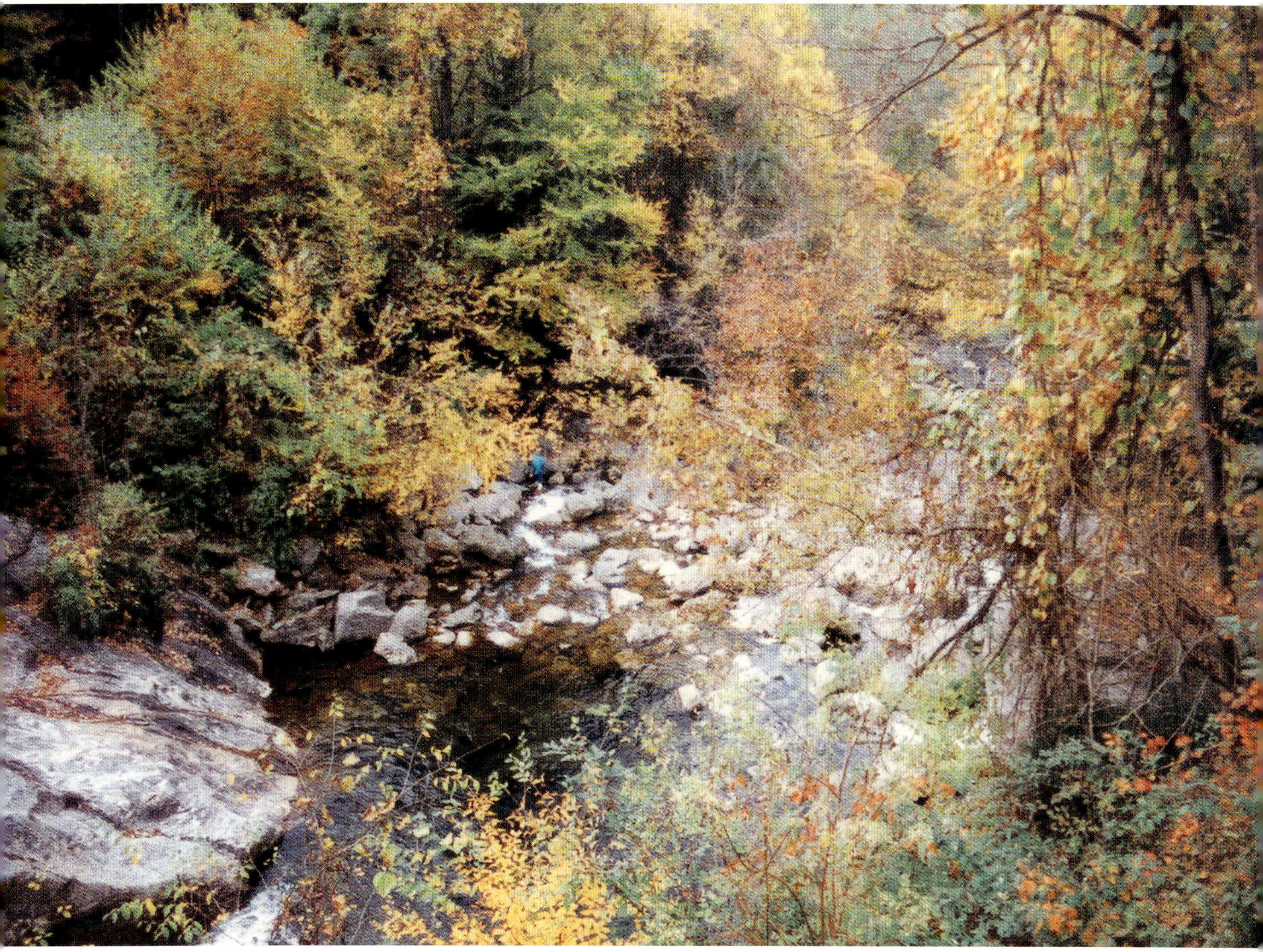

out of the brook

2 Samuel 23 : 1-5

Now these *be* the last words of David.
David the son of Jesse said, and the man *who was* raised up on high,
the anointed of the God of Jacob, and the sweet psalmist of Israel, said,

The Spirit of the LORD spake by me, and his word *was* in my tongue.

The God of Israel said, the Rock of Israel spake to me,
HE THAT RULETH OVER MEN *MUST BE* JUST,
RULING IN THE FEAR OF GOD.

AND *HE SHALL BE* AS THE LIGHT OF THE MORNING,
WHEN THE SUN RISETH,
EVEN A MORNING WITHOUT CLOUDS;
AS THE TENDER GRASS *SPRINGING* OUT OF THE EARTH
BY CLEAR SHINING AFTER RAIN.

Although my house *be* not so with God;
yet he hath made with me an everlasting covenant,
ordered in all *things*, and sure:
for *this is* all my salvation, and all *my* desire,
although he make *it* not to grow.

AS THE TENDER GRASS

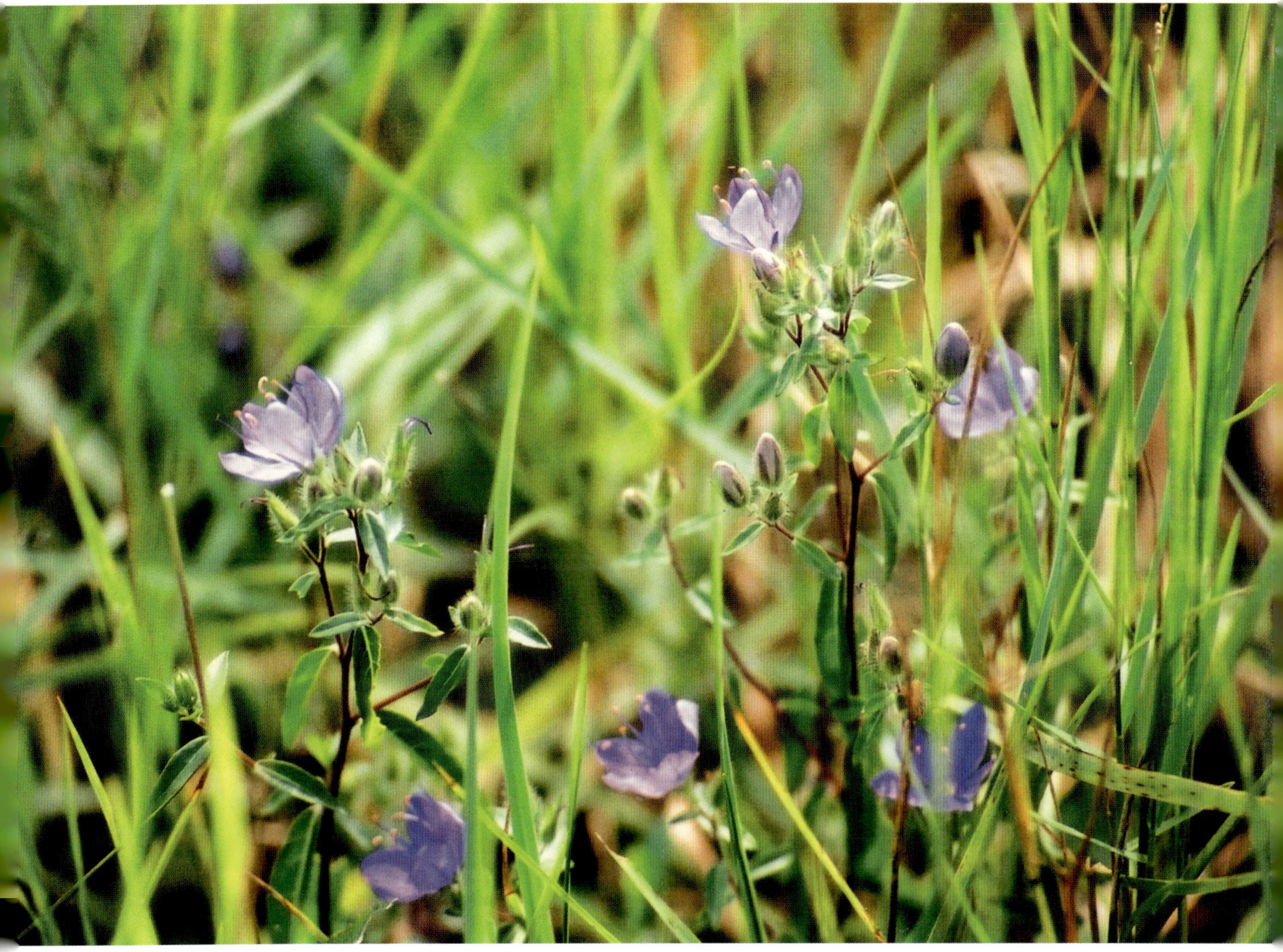

SPRINGING OUT OF THE EARTH

1 Kings 14 : 15-16

For the LORD shall smite Israel,
as a reed is shaken in the water,
and he shall root up Israel out of this good land,
which he gave to their fathers,
and shall scatter them beyond the river,
because they have made their groves,
provoking the LORD to anger.

And he shall give Israel up because of the sins of Jeroboam,
who did sin,
and who made Israel to sin.

and shall scatter them

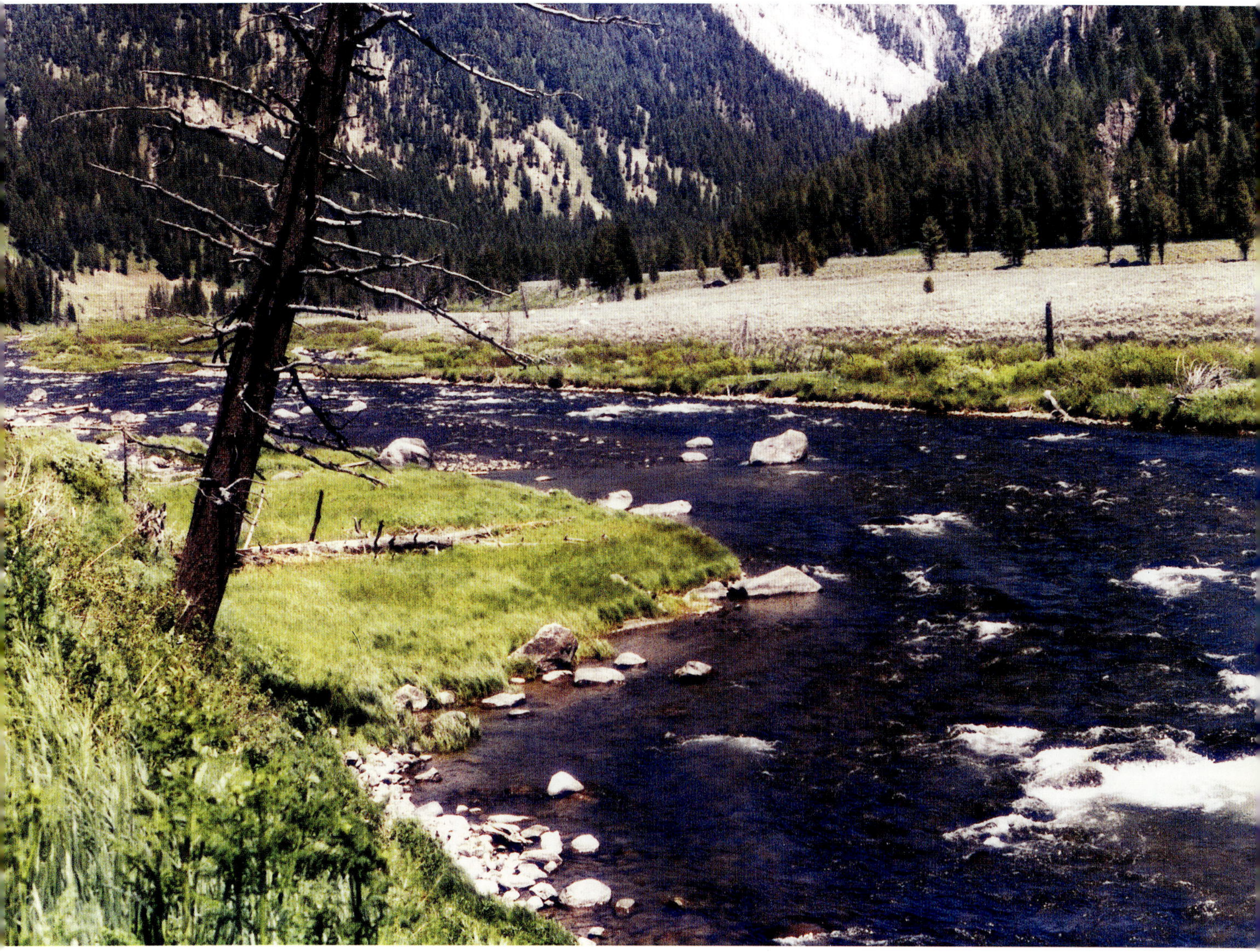

beyond the river

2 Kings 2 : 11-13

And it came to pass,
as they still went on, and talked,
that, behold,
there appeared a chariot of fire,
and horses of fire,
and parted them both asunder;
and Elijah went up by a whirlwind into heaven.

And Elisha saw *it*, and he cried,
My father, my father,
the chariot of Israel,
and the horsemen thereof.
And he saw him no more:
and he took hold of his own clothes,
and rent them in two pieces.

He took up also the mantle of Elijah that fell from him,
and went back, and stood by the bank of Jordan;

and Elijah went up by a whirlwind

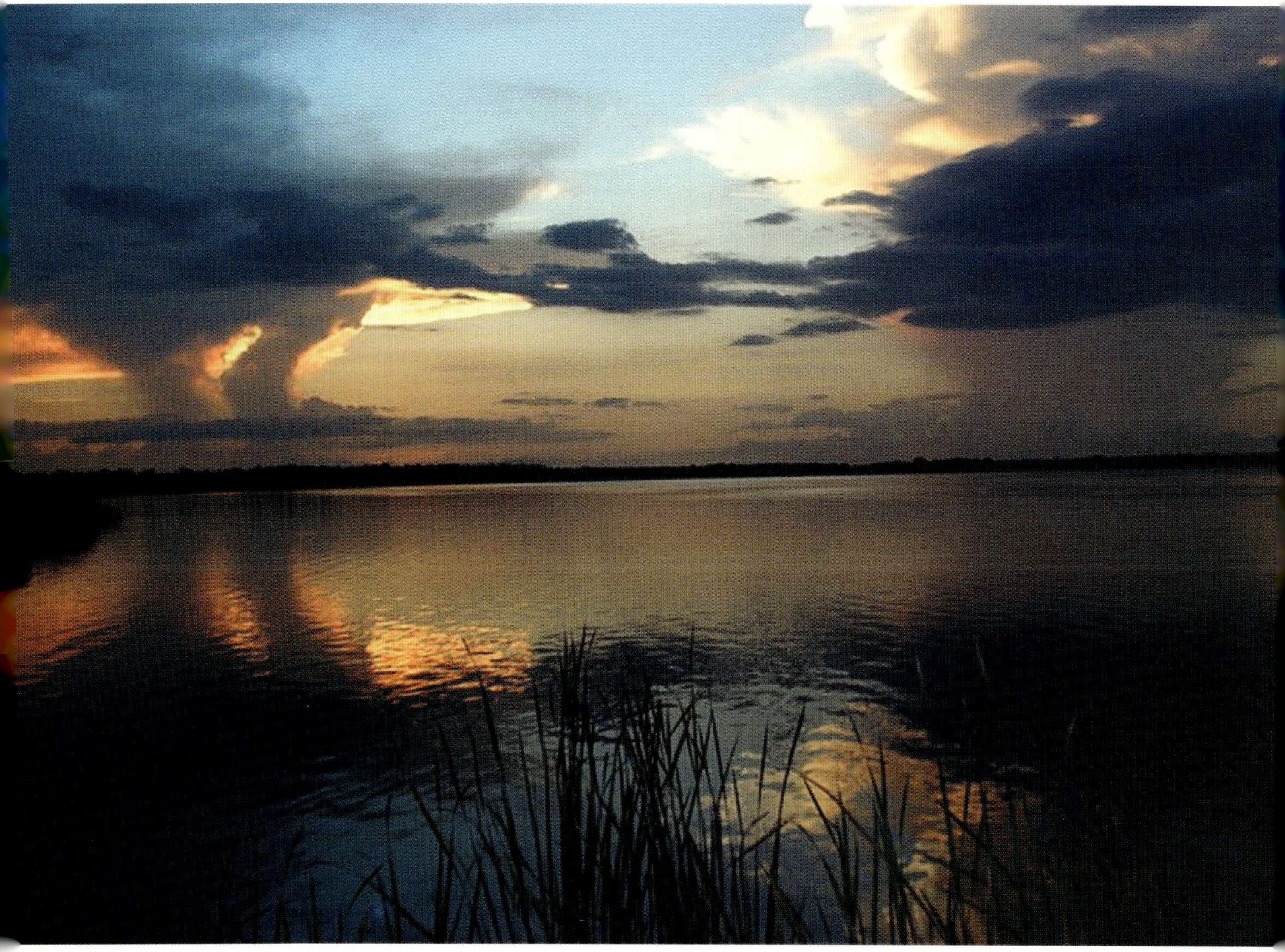

into heaven

1 Chronicles 16 : 23-32

Sing unto the LORD, all the earth; shew forth from day to day his salvation.

Declare his glory among the heathen; his marvellous works among all nations.

For great *is* the LORD, and greatly to be praised: he also *is* to be feared above all gods.

For all the gods of the people *are* idols: but the LORD made the heavens.

Glory and honour *are* in his presence; strength and gladness *are* in his place.

Give unto the LORD, ye kindreds of the people, give unto the LORD glory and strength.

Give unto the LORD the glory *due* unto his name:
bring an offering, and come before him:
worship the LORD in the beauty of holiness.

Fear before him, all the earth: the world also shall be stable, that it be not moved.

Let the heavens be glad, and let the earth rejoice:
and let *men* say among the nations, The LORD reigneth.

Let the sea roar, and the fulness thereof: let the fields rejoice, and all that *is* therein.

Let the sea roar, and the fulness thereof:

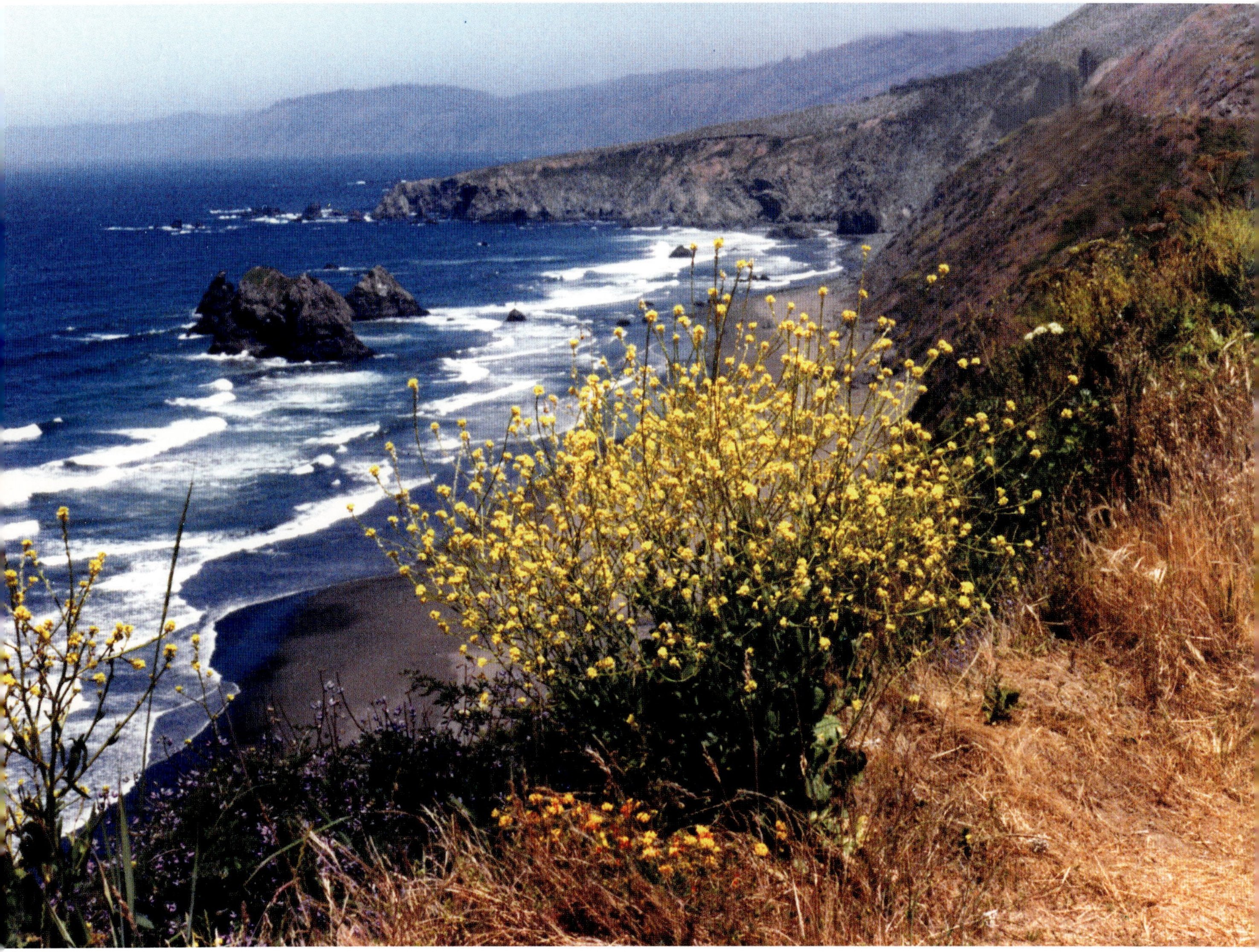

let the fields rejoice, and all that *is* therein

2 Chronicles 25 : 18-20

And Joash king of Israel sent to Amaziah king of Judah,
saying,
The thistle that *was* in Lebanon sent to the cedar that *was* in Lebanon,
saying,
Give thy daughter to my son to wife:
and there passed by a wild beast that *was* in Lebanon,
and trode down the thistle.

Thou sayest,
Lo, thou hast smitten the Edomites;
and thine heart lifteth thee up to boast:
abide now at home;
why shouldest thou meddle to *thine* hurt,
that thou shouldest fall,
even thou,
and Judah with thee?

But Amaziah would not hear;
for it *came* of God,
that he might deliver them into the hand *of their enemies,*
because they sought after the gods of Edom.

The thistle that *was* in Lebanon

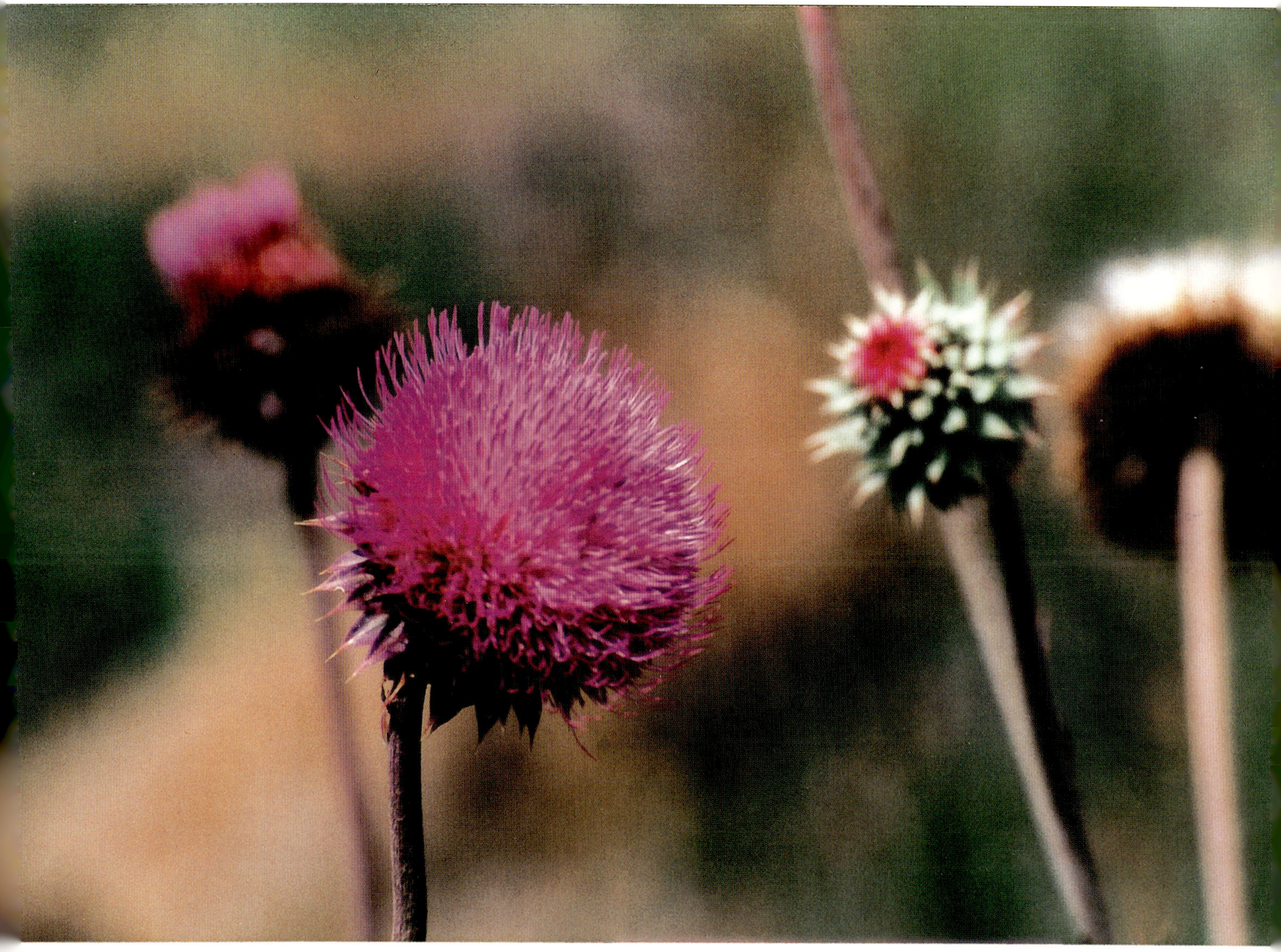

sent to the cedar that *was* in Lebanon

Ezra 8 : 21-23

Then I proclaimed a fast there, at the river of Ahava,
that we might afflict ourselves before our God,
to seek of him a right way for us,
and for our little ones,
and for all our substance.

For I was ashamed to require of the king a band of soldiers and horsemen
to help us against the enemy in the way:
because we had spoken unto the king,
saying,
The hand of our God *is* upon all them for good that seek him;
but his power and his wrath *is* against all them that forsake him.

So we fasted and besought our God for this:
and he was intreated of us.

Then I proclaimed a fast there,

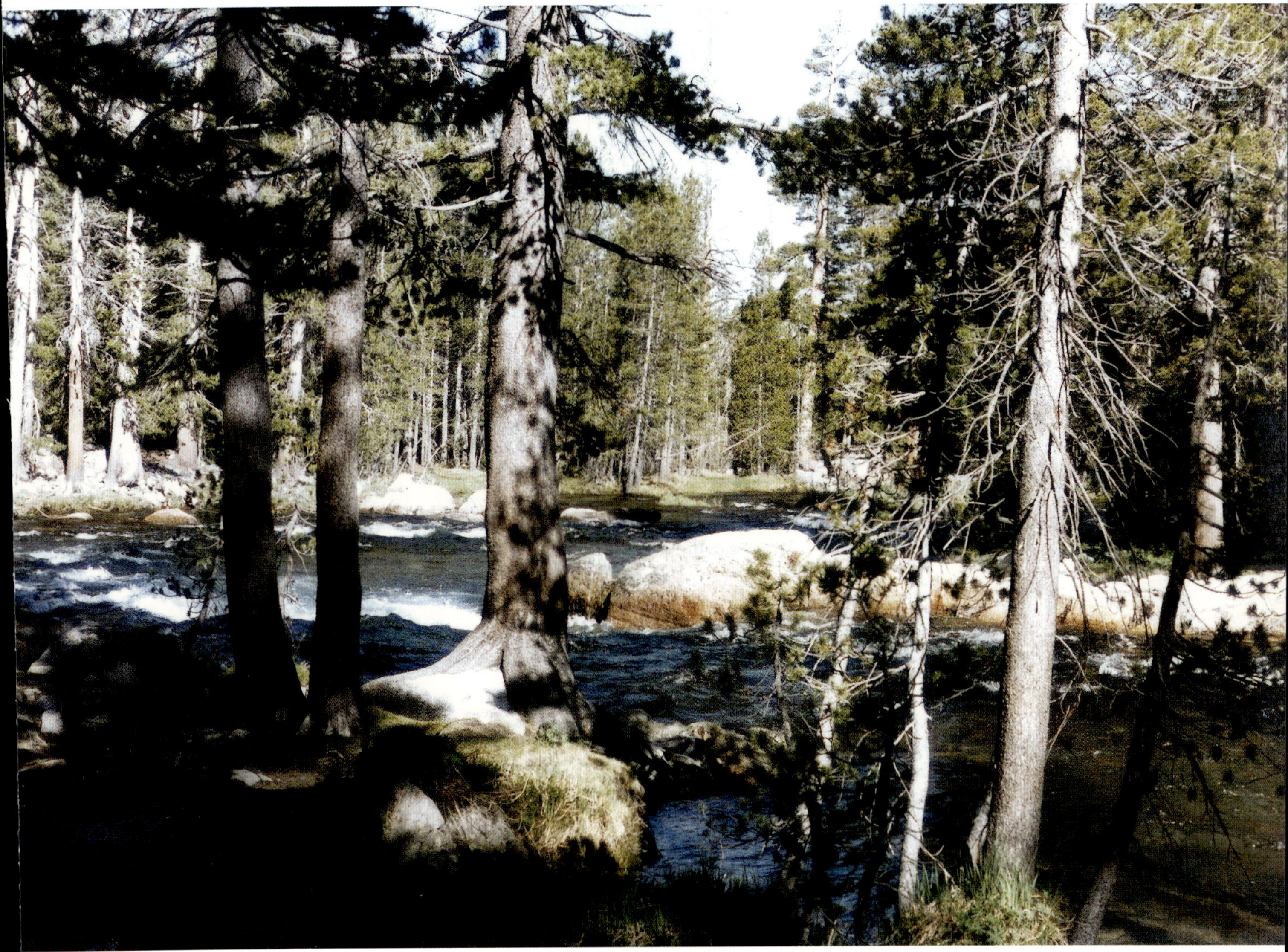

at the river of Ahava

Nevertheless they were disobedient,
and rebelled against thee,
and cast thy law behind their backs,
and slew thy prophets which testified against them to turn them to thee,
and they wrought great provocations.

Therefore thou deliveredst them into the hand of their enemies,
who vexed them:
and in the time of their trouble,
when they cried unto thee,
thou heardest *them* from heaven;
and according to thy manifold mercies thou gavest them saviours,
who saved them out of the hand of their enemies.

thou heardest *them*

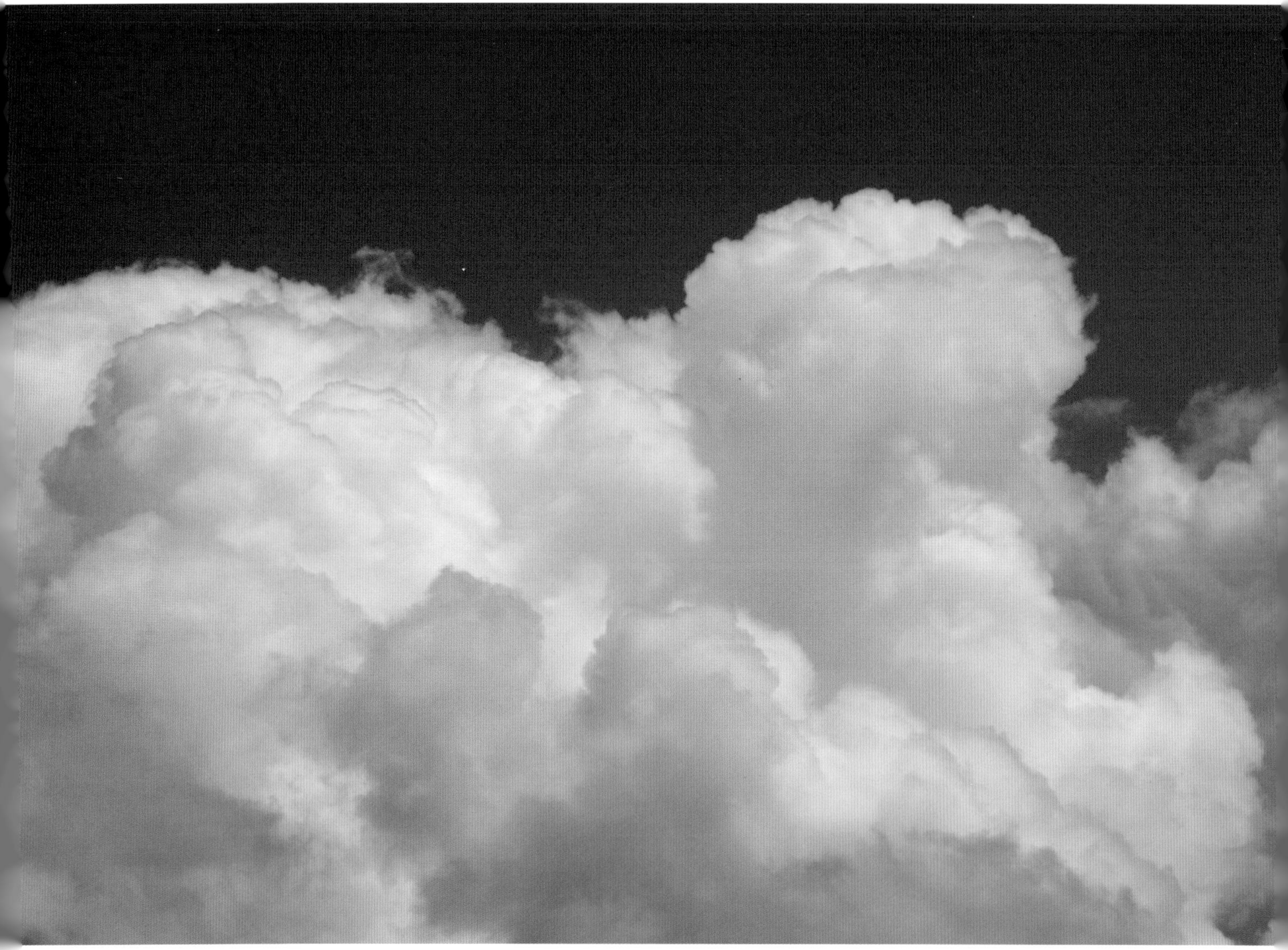

from heaven

Esther 7 : 4-8

For we are sold, I and my people,
to be destroyed, to be slain, and to perish.
But if we had been sold for bondmen and bondwomen,
I had held my tongue,
although the enemy could not countervail the king's damage.

Then the king Ahasuerus answered and said unto Esther the queen,
Who is he, and where is he, that durst presume in his heart to do so?

And Esther said, The adversary and enemy *is* this wicked Haman.
Then Haman was afraid before the king and the queen.

And the king arising from the banquet of wine
in his wrath *went* into the palace garden:
and Haman stood up to make request for his life to Esther the queen;
for he saw that there was evil determined against him by the king.

Then the king returned out of the palace garden
into the place of the banquet of wine;
and Haman was fallen upon the bed whereon Esther *was*.
Then said the king, Will he force the queen also before me in the house?
As the word went out of the king's mouth, they covered Haman's face.

Then the king returned out of the palace garden

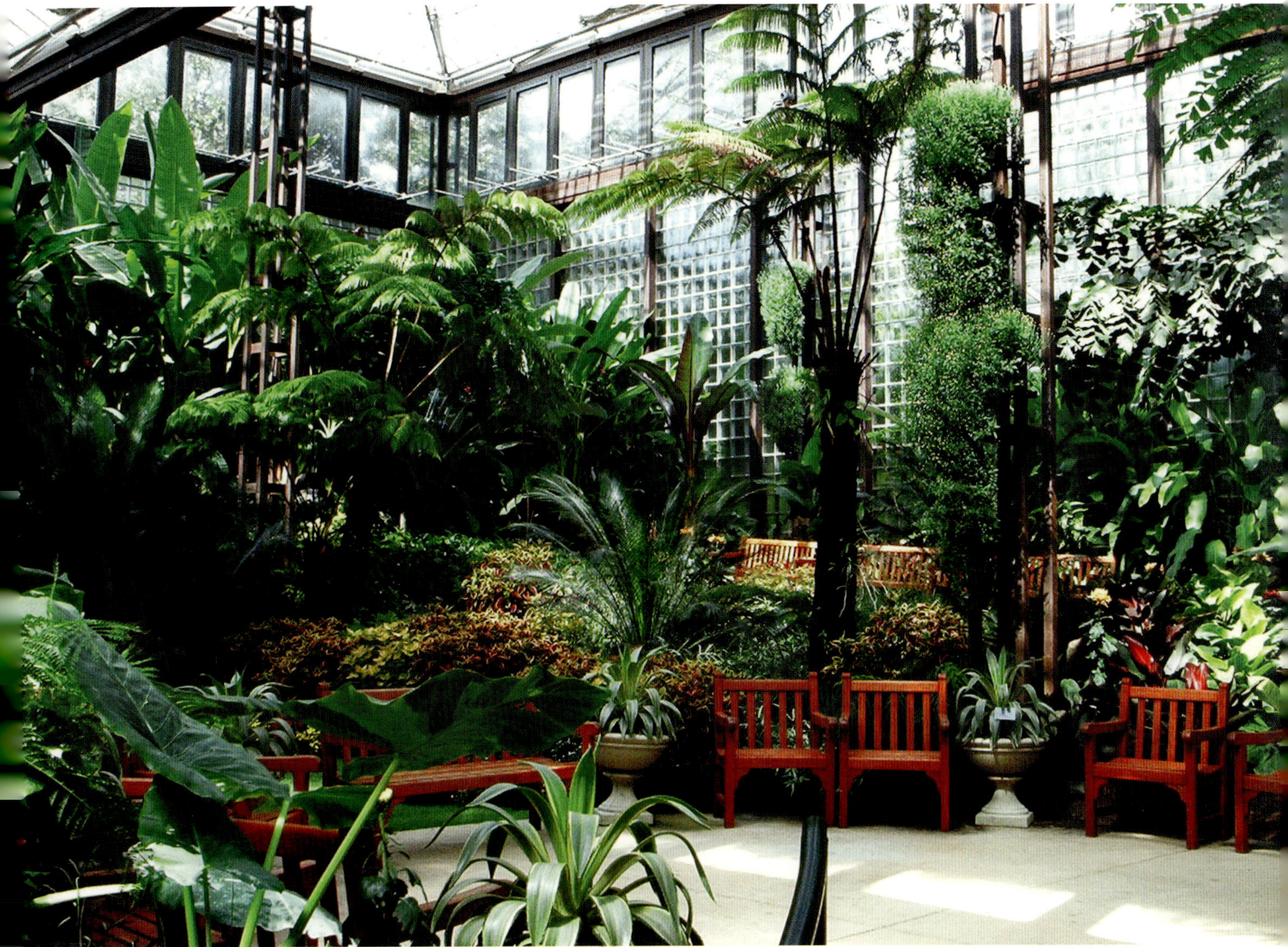

Photo: John A. Sibley Horticultural Center, Callaway Gardens, Pine Mountain, GA

into the place of the banquet of wine

Job 19 : 7-8

Behold,
I cry out of wrong,
but I am not heard:
I cry aloud,
but *there is* no judgement.
He hath fenced up my way that I cannot pass,
and he hath set darkness in my paths.

Job 19: 23-27

Oh that my words were now written!
oh that they were printed in a book!

That they were graven with an iron pen and lead in the rock for ever!

For I know *that* my redeemer liveth,
and *that* he shall stand at the latter *day* upon the earth:

And *though* after my skin *worms* destroy this *body*,
yet in my flesh shall I see God:

Whom I shall see for myself,
and mine eyes shall behold,
and not another;
though my reins be consumed within me.

He hath fenced up my way that I cannot pass,

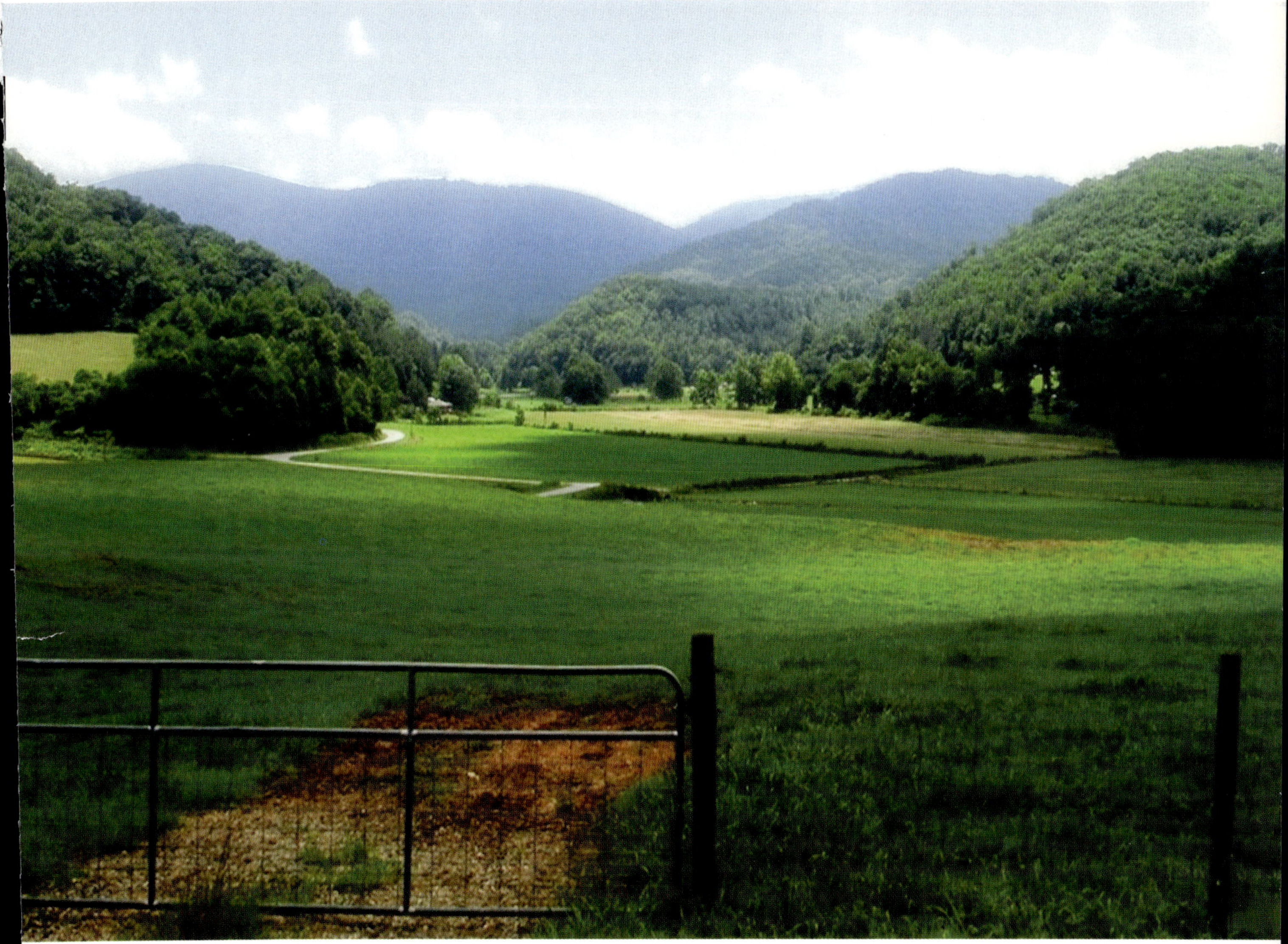

and he hath set darkness in my paths

Psalm 103 : 15-19

As for man, his days *are* as grass:
as a flower of the field, so he flourisheth.

For the wind passeth over it, and it is gone;
and the place thereof shall know it no more.

But the mercy of the LORD *is* from everlasting
to everlasting upon them that fear him,
and his righteousness unto children's children;

To such as keep his covenant,
and to those that remember his commandments to do them.

The LORD hath prepared his throne in the heavens;
and his kingdom ruleth over all.

as a flower of the field,

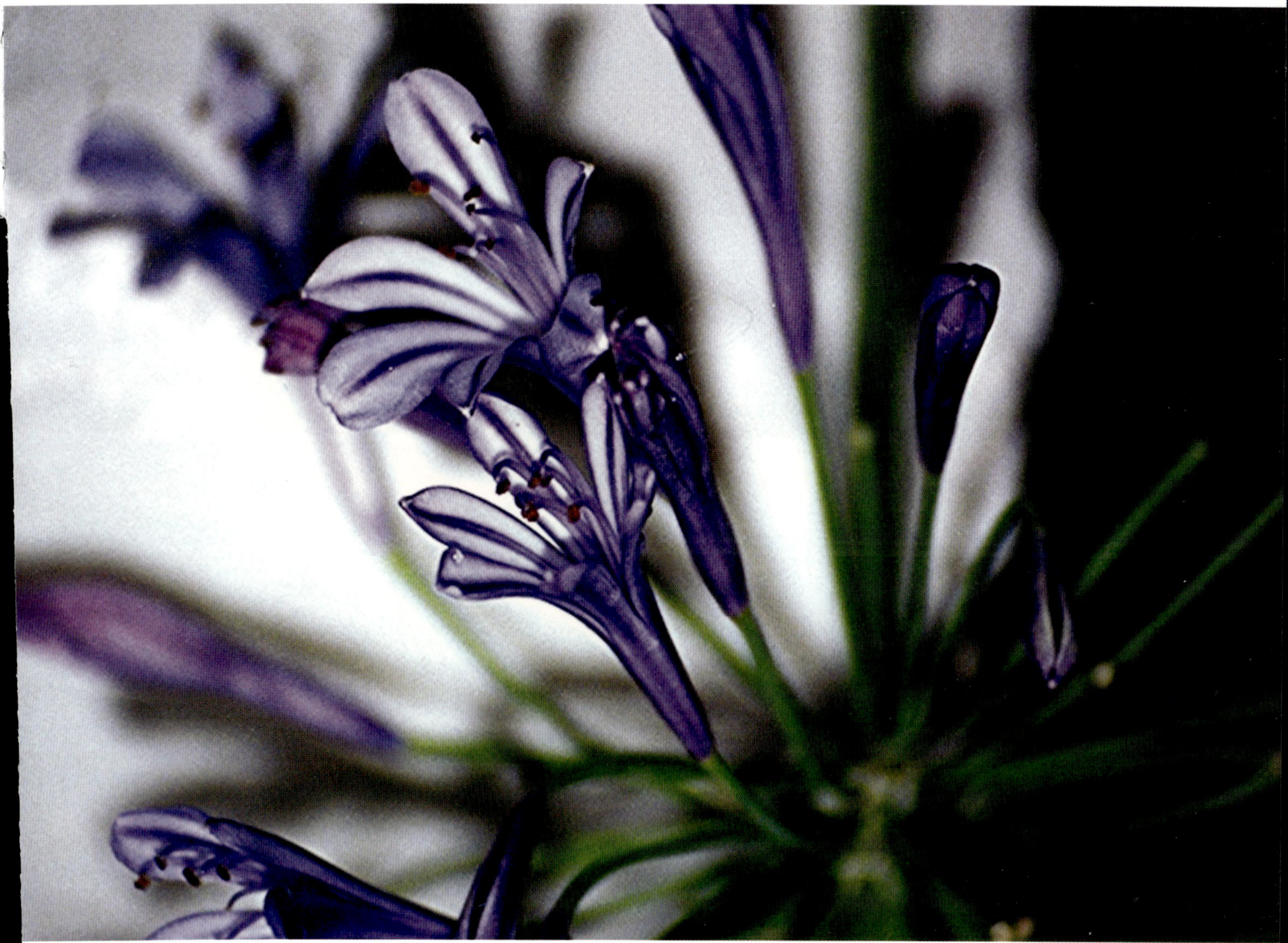

so he flourisheth

Proverbs 3 : 1-8

My son, forget not my law;
but let thine heart keep my commandments:

For length of days, and long life, and peace,
shall they add to thee.

Let not mercy and truth forsake thee:
bind them about thy neck;
write them upon the table of thine heart:

So shalt thou find favour and good understanding
in the sight of God and man.

Trust in the LORD with all thine heart;
and lean not unto thine own understanding.

In all thy ways acknowledge him,
and he shall direct thy paths.

Be not wise in thine own eyes:
fear the LORD, and depart from evil.

It shall be health to thy navel, and marrow to thy bones.

and
he
shall
direct

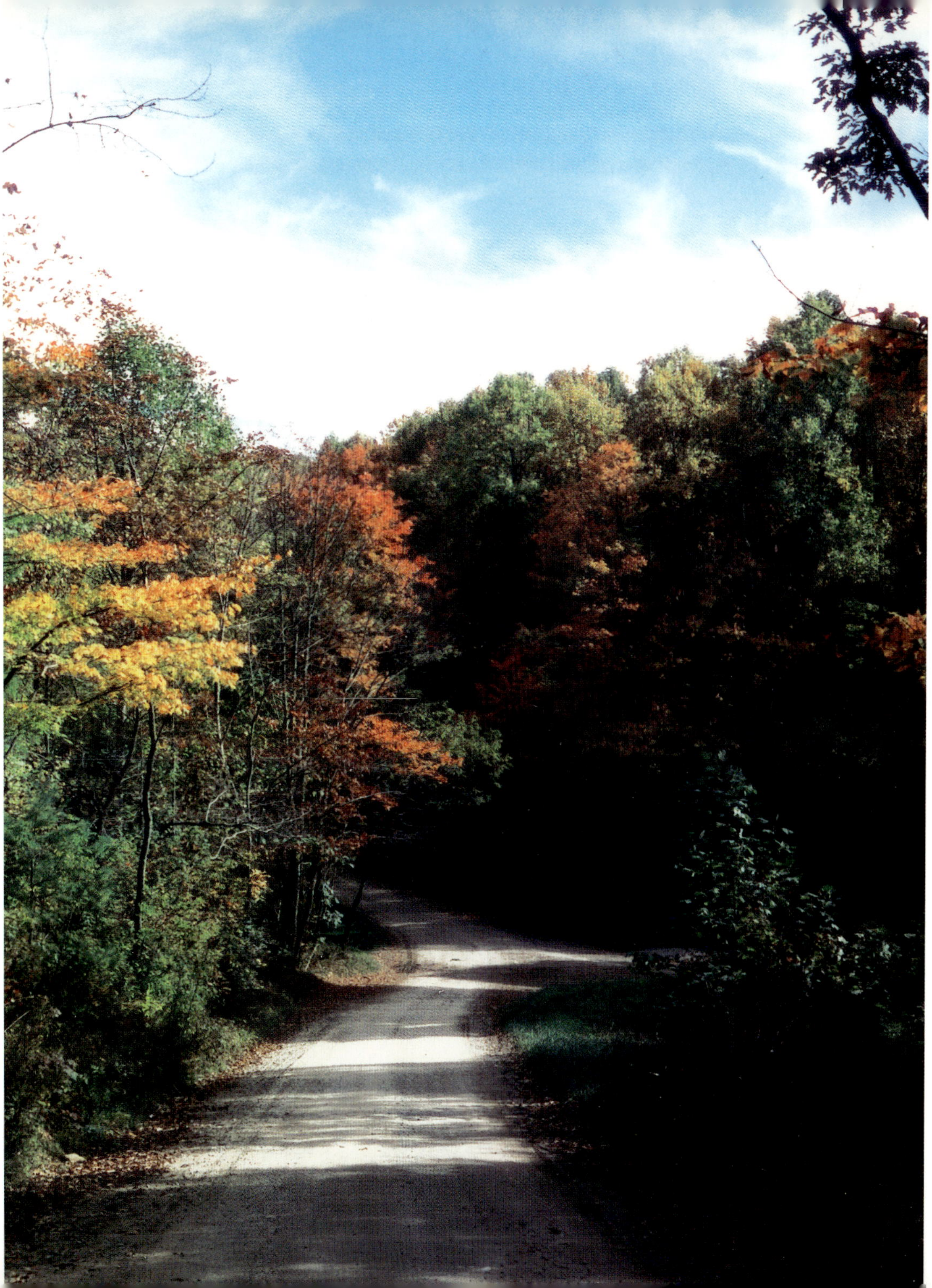

thy
paths

Ecclesiastes 3 : 1-11

To every *thing there is* a season, and a time to every purpose under the heaven:
A time to be born, and a time to die;
a time to plant, and a time to pluck up *that which is* planted;
A time to kill, and a time to heal;
a time to break down, and a time to build up;
A time to weep, and a time to laugh;
a time to mourn, and a time to dance;
A time to cast away stones, and a time to gather stones together;
a time to embrace, and a time to refrain from embracing;
A time to get, and a time to lose;
a time to keep, and a time to cast away;
A time to rend, and a time to sew;
a time to keep silence, and a time to speak;
A time to love, and a time to hate;
a time of war, and a time of peace.

What profit hath he that worketh in that wherein he laboureth?
I have seen the travail,
which God hath given to the sons of men to be exercised in it.

He hath made every *thing* beautiful in his time:
also he hath set the world in their heart,
so that no man can find out the work that God maketh from the beginning to the end.

he hath made every *thing* beautiful

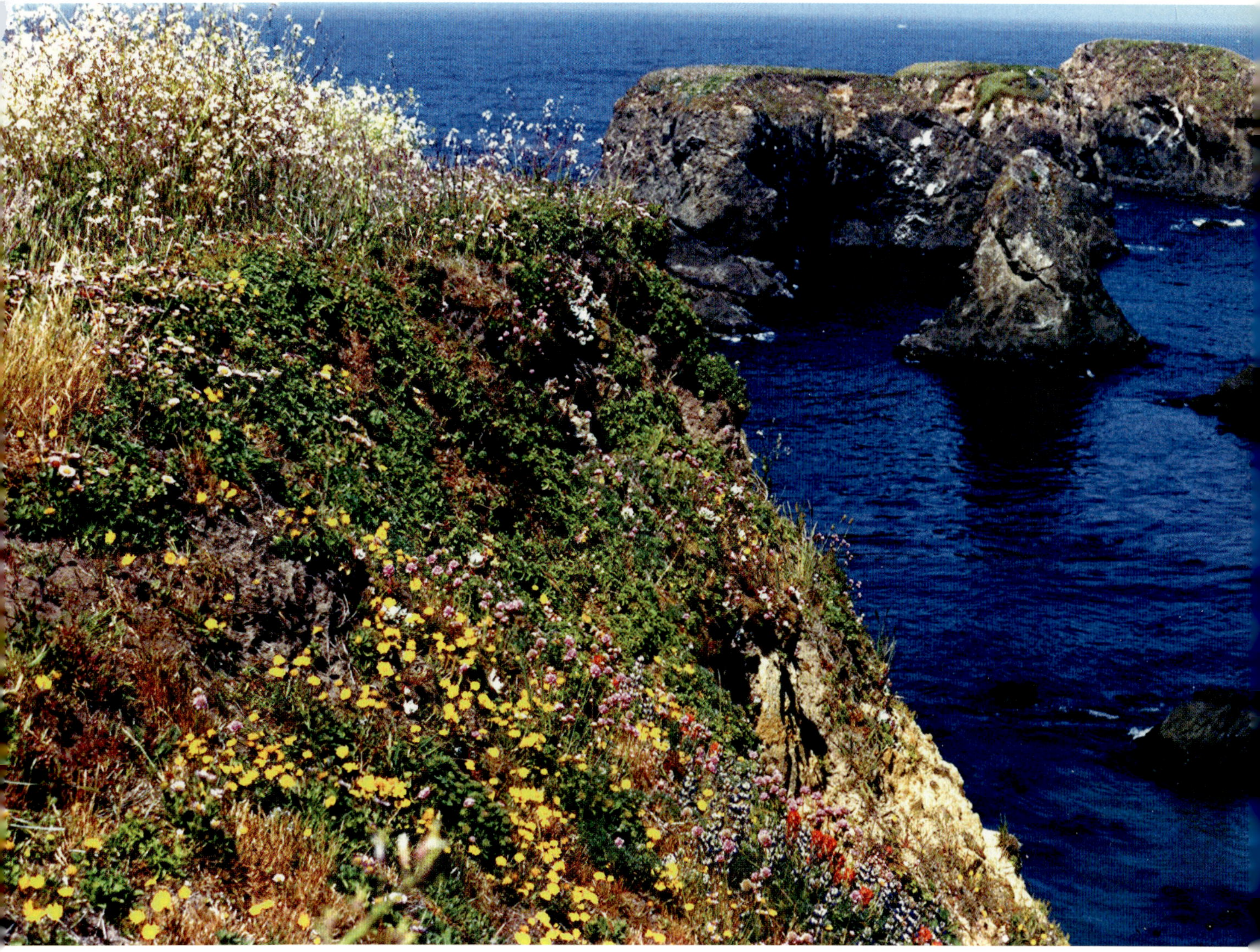

in his time

Song of Solomon 2 : 10-13

My beloved spake,
and said unto me,
Rise up,
my love,
my fair one,
and come away.

For, lo,
the winter is past,
the rain is over *and* gone;

The flowers appear on the earth;
the time of of singing *of birds* is come,
and the voice of the turtle is heard in our land;

The fig tree putteth forth her green figs,
and the vines *with* the tender grape give a *good* smell.
Arise,
my love,
my fair one,
and come away.

The flowers appear

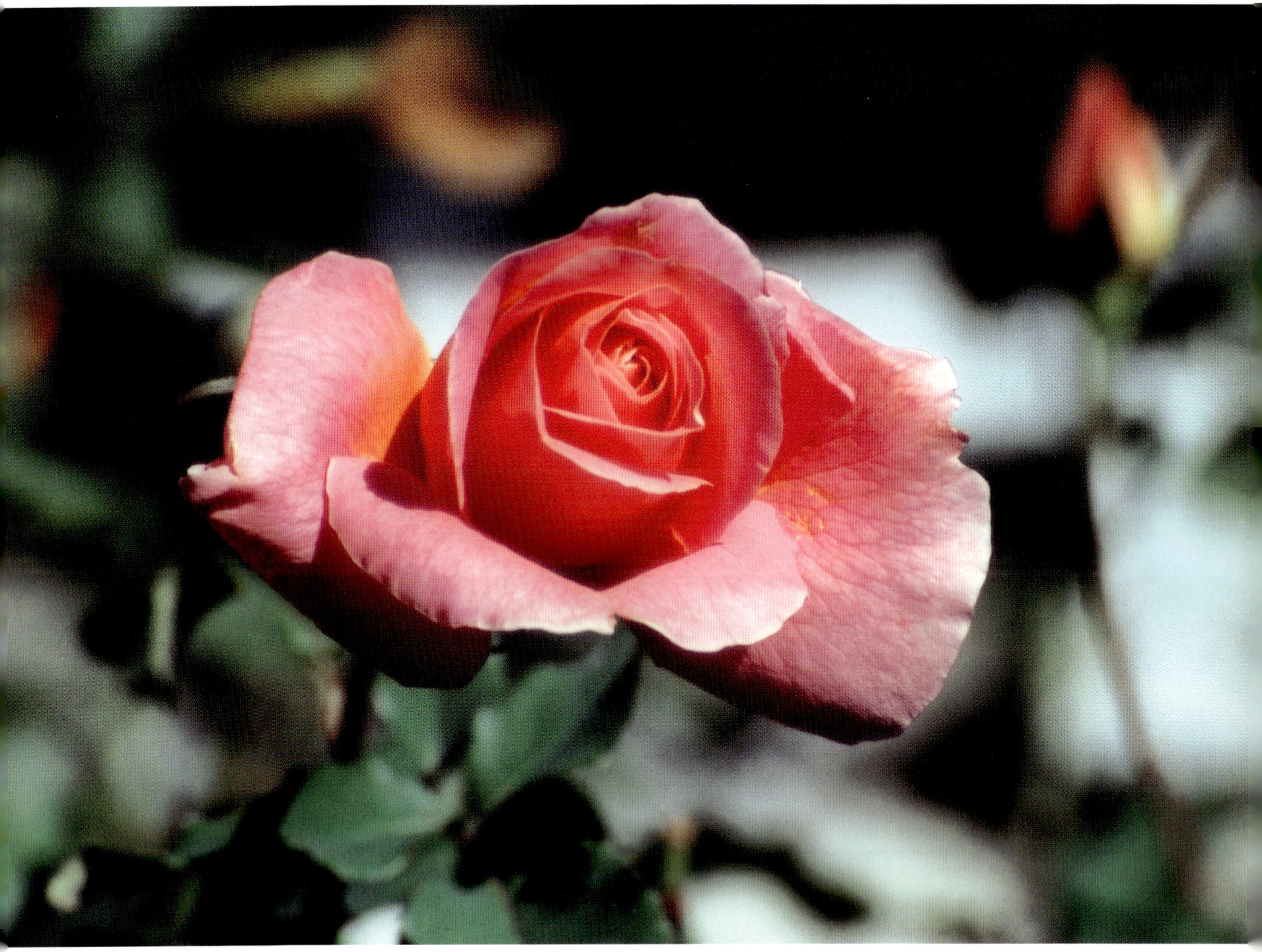

on the earth

Isaiah 1 : 15-18

AND WHEN YE SPREAD FORTH YOUR HANDS,
I WILL HIDE MINE EYES FROM YOU:
YEA, WHEN YE MAKE MANY PRAYERS,
I WILL NOT HEAR:
YOUR HANDS ARE FULL OF BLOOD.

WASH YOU,
MAKE YOU CLEAN;
PUT AWAY THE EVIL OF YOUR DOINGS FROM BEFORE MINE EYES;
CEASE TO DO EVIL;

LEARN TO DO WELL;
SEEK JUDGEMENT,
RELIEVE THE OPPRESSED,
JUDGE THE FATHERLESS,
PLEAD FOR THE WIDOW.

COME NOW,
AND LET US REASON TOGETHER,
saith the LORD:
THOUGH YOUR SINS BE AS SCARLET,
THEY SHALL BE AS WHITE AS SNOW;
THOUGH THEY BE RED LIKE CRIMSON,
THEY SHALL BE AS WOOL.

THOUGH YOUR SINS BE AS SCARLET,

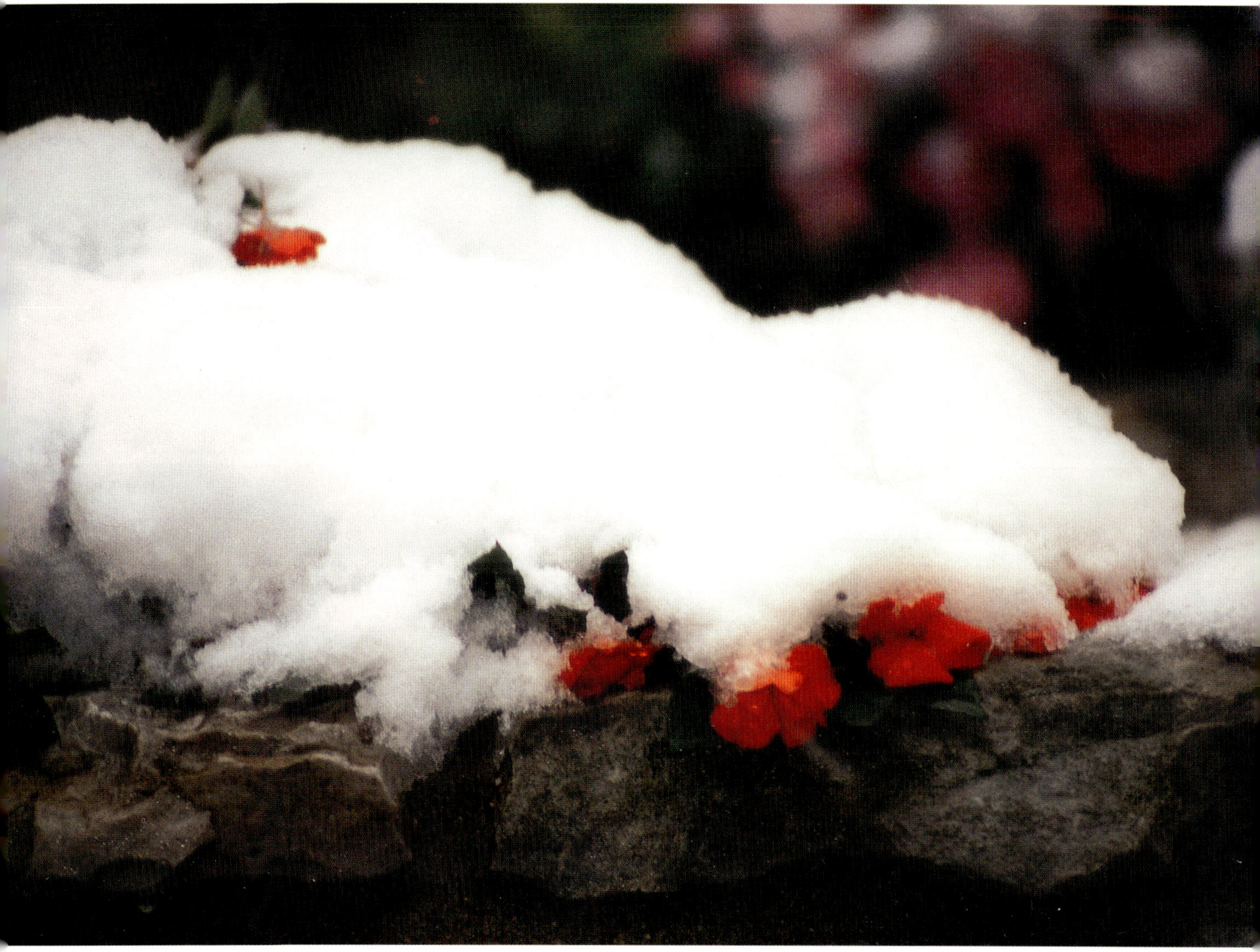

THEY SHALL BE AS WHITE AS SNOW

Jeremiah 12 : 10-12

MANY PASTORS HAVE DESTROYED MY VINEYARD,
THEY HAVE TRODDEN MY PORTION UNDER FOOT,
THEY HAVE MADE MY PLEASANT PORTION A DESOLATE WILDERNESS.

THEY HAVE MADE IT DESOLATE,
AND BEING DESOLATE IT MOURNETH UNTO ME;
THE WHOLE LAND IS MADE DESOLATE,
BECAUSE NO MAN LAYETH *IT* TO HEART.

THE SPOILERS ARE COME UPON ALL HIGH PLACES THROUGH THE WILDERNESS:
FOR THE SWORD OF THE LORD SHALL DEVOUR FROM THE *ONE* END OF THE LAND
EVEN TO THE *OTHER* END OF THE LAND:
NO FLESH SHALL HAVE PEACE.

THE SPOILERS ARE COME UPON ALL HIGH PLACES

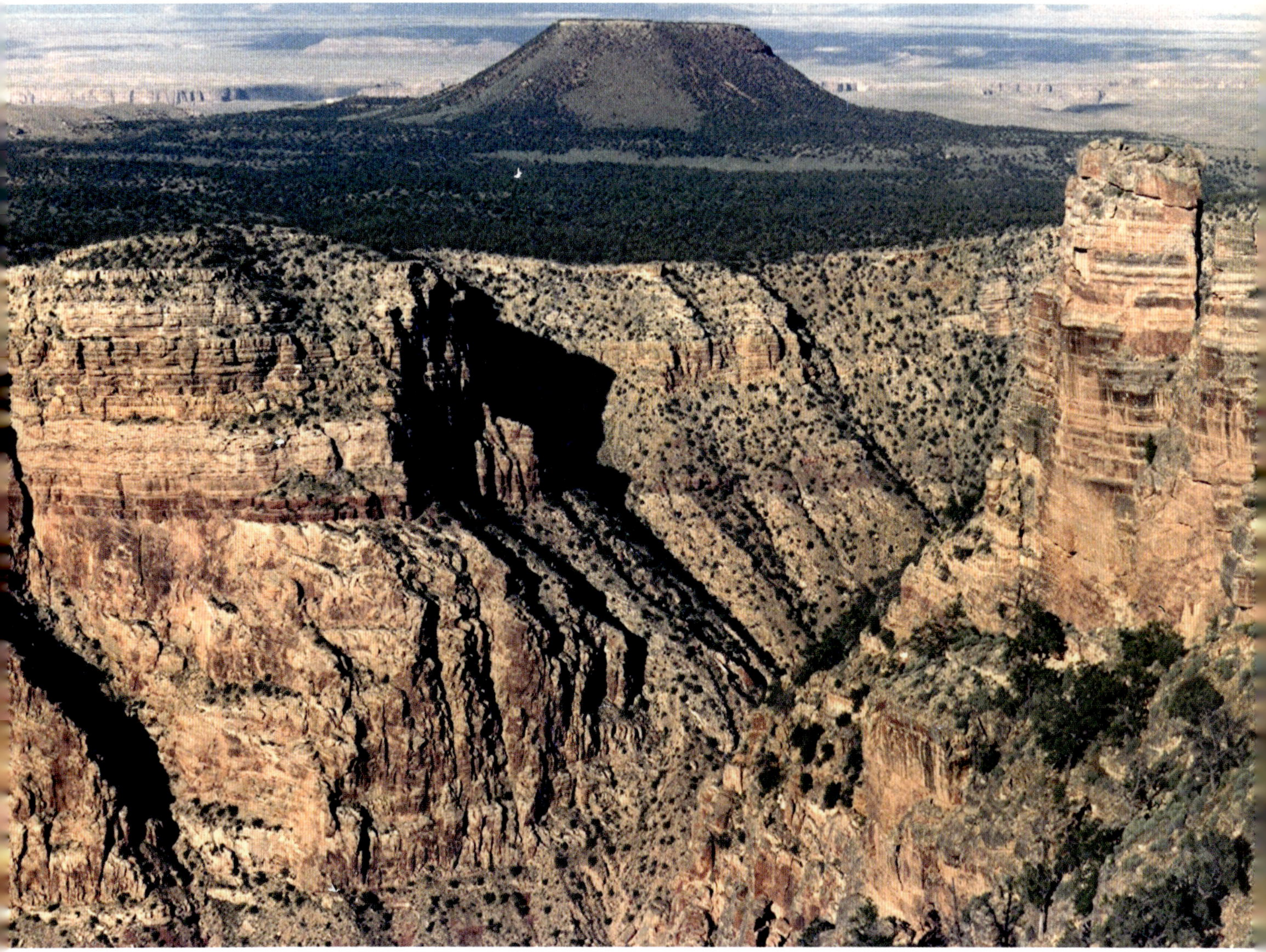

THROUGH THE WILDERNESS

Lamentations 5 : 15-22

The joy of our heart is ceased;
our dance is turned into mourning.

The crown is fallen *from* our head:
woe unto us, that we have sinned!

For this our heart is faint;
for these *things* our eyes are dim.

Because of the mountain of Zion,
which is desolate, the foxes walk upon it.

Thou, O LORD, remainest for ever;
thy throne from generation to generation.

Wherefore dost thou forget us for ever,
and forsake us so long time?

Turn thou us unto thee, O LORD,
and we shall be turned;
renew our days as of old.

But thou hast utterly rejected us;
thou art very wroth against us.

renew
our
days

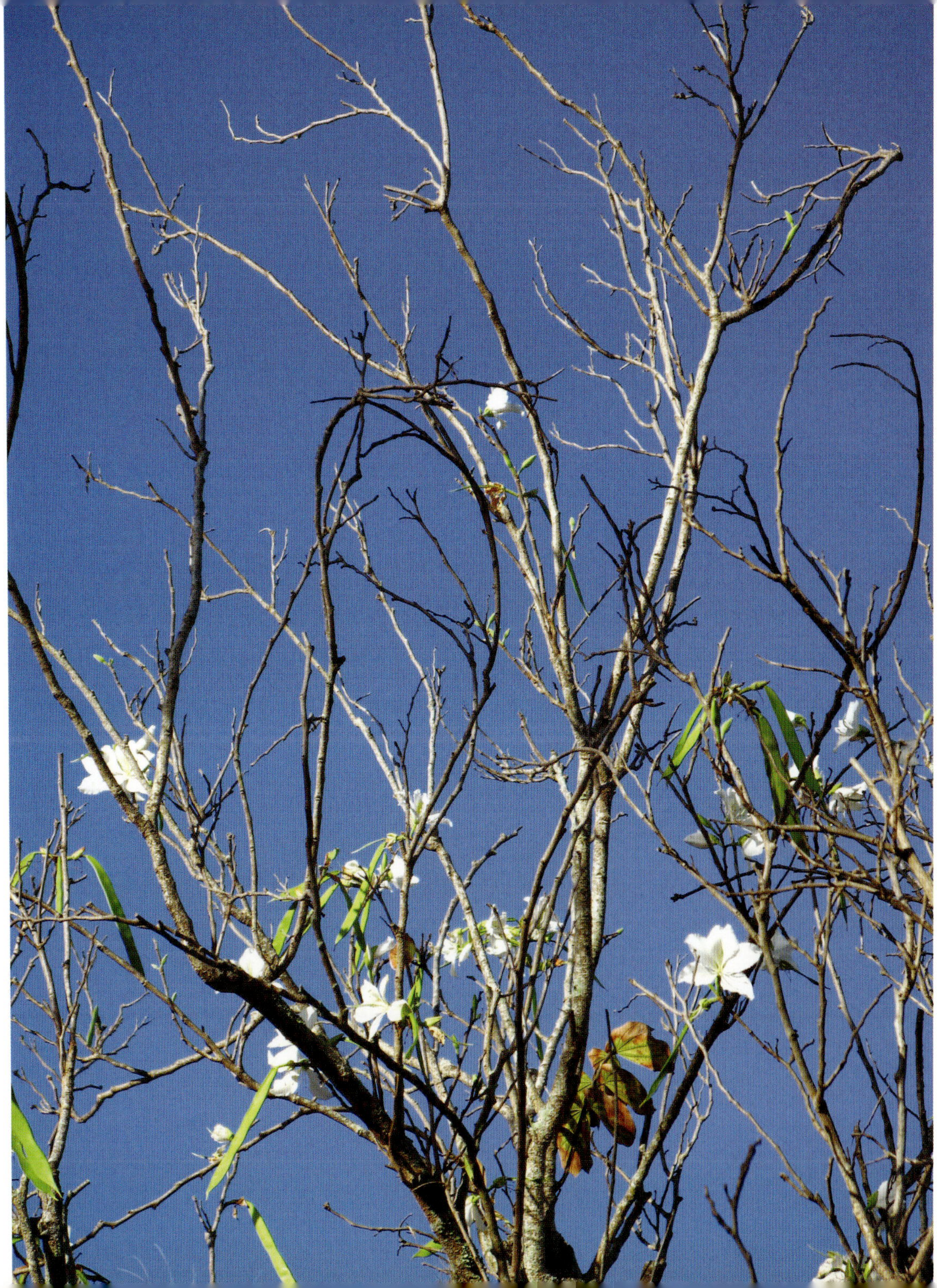

as
of
old

Ezekiel 36 : 26-30

A NEW HEART ALSO WILL I GIVE YOU,
AND A NEW SPIRIT WILL I PUT WITHIN YOU:
AND I WILL TAKE AWAY THE STONY HEART OUT OF YOUR FLESH,
AND I WILL GIVE YOU AN HEART OF FLESH.

AND I WILL PUT MY SPIRIT WITHIN YOU,
AND CAUSE YOU TO WALK IN MY STATUTES,
AND YE SHALL KEEP MY JUDGEMENTS,
AND DO *THEM.*

AND YE SHALL DWELL IN THE LAND THAT I GAVE TO YOUR FATHERS;
AND YE SHALL BE MY PEOPLE,
AND I WILL BE YOUR GOD.

I WILL ALSO SAVE YOU FROM ALL YOUR UNCLEANNESSES:
AND I WILL CALL FOR THE CORN,
AND WILL INCREASE IT,
AND LAY NO FAMINE UPON YOU.

AND I WILL MULTIPLY THE FRUIT OF THE TREE,
AND THE INCREASE OF THE FIELD,
THAT YE SHALL RECEIVE NO MORE REPROACH OF FAMINE AMONG THE HEATHEN.

AND I WILL MULTIPLY

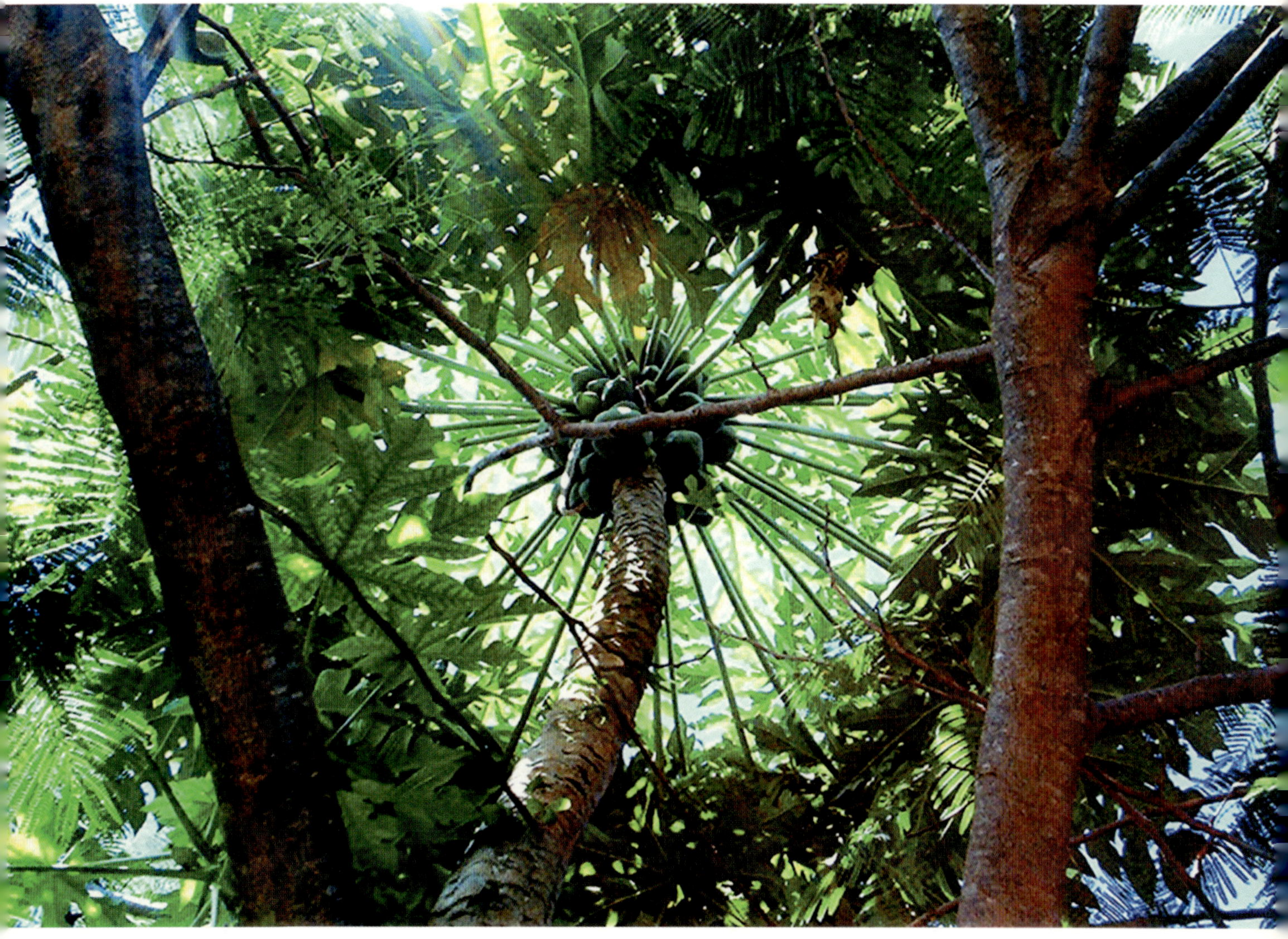

THE FRUIT OF THE TREE

Daniel 2 : 19-23

Then was the secret revealed unto Daniel in a night vision.
Then Daniel blessed the God of heaven.

Daniel answered and said,
Blessed be the name of God for ever and ever:
for wisdom and might are his:

And he changeth the times and the seasons:
he removeth kings,
and setteth up kings:
he giveth wisdom unto the wise,
and knowledge to them that know understanding:

He revealeth the deep and secret things:
he knoweth what *is* in the darkness,
and the light dwelleth with him.

I thank thee, and praise thee,
O thou God of my fathers,
who hast given me wisdom and might,
and hast made known unto me now what we desired of thee:
for thou has *now* made known unto us the king's matter.

and
he
c
h
a
n
g
e
t
h
the
times

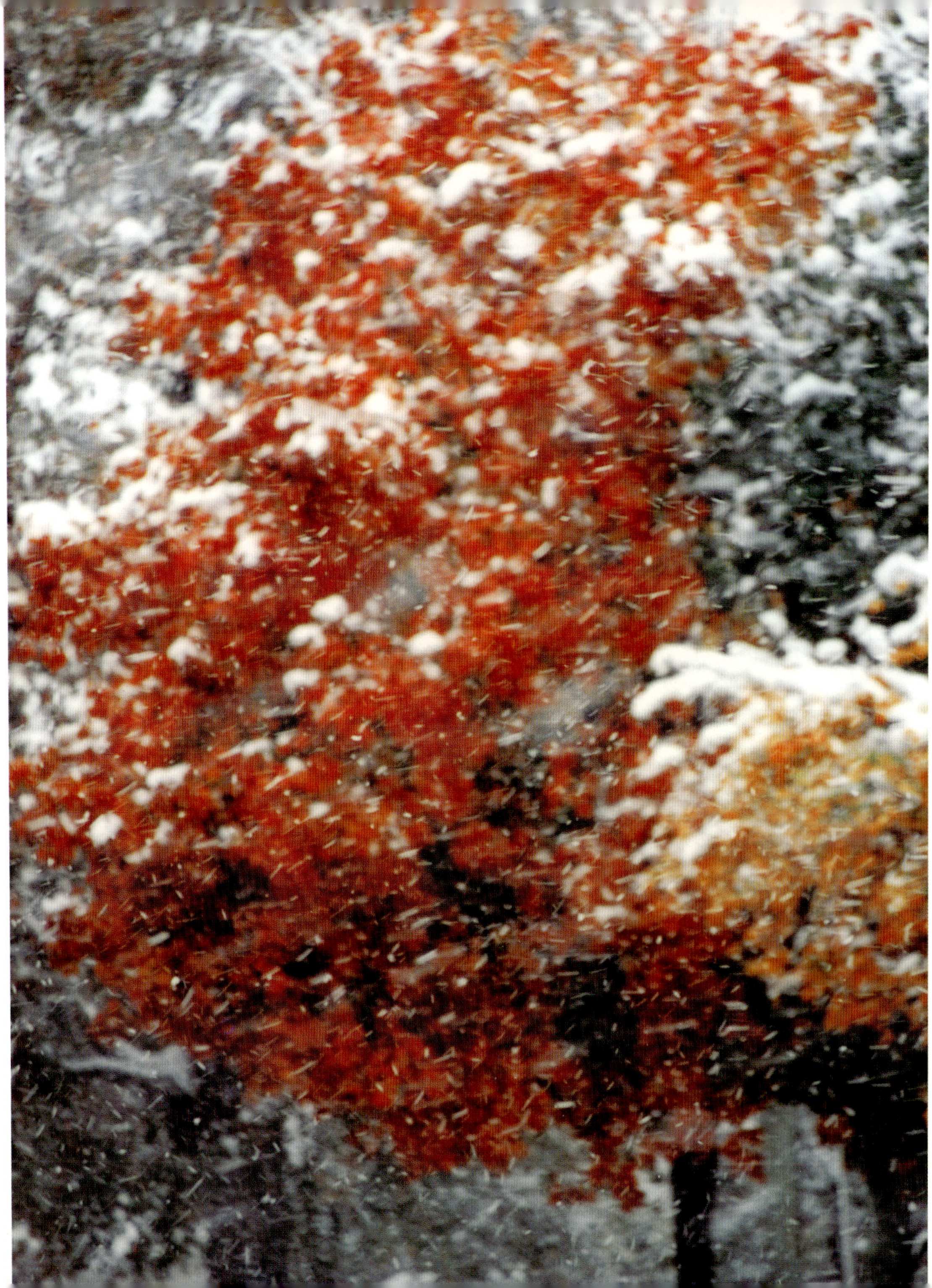

and
the
seasons

Hosea 14 : 4-8

I WILL HEAL THEIR BACKSLIDING,
I WILL LOVE THEM FREELY;
FOR MINE ANGER IS TURNED AWAY FROM HIM.

I WILL BE AS THE DEW UNTO ISRAEL:
HE SHALL GROW AS THE LILY,
AND CAST FORTH HIS ROOTS AS LEBANON.

HIS BRANCHES SHALL SPREAD,
AND HIS BEAUTY SHALL BE AS THE OLIVE TREE,
AND HIS SMELL AS LEBANON.

THEY THAT DWELL UNDER HIS SHADOW SHALL RETURN;
THEY SHALL REVIVE *AS* THE CORN,
AND GROW AS THE VINE:
THE SCENT THEREOF *SHALL BE* AS THE WINE OF LEBANON.

EPHRAIM *SHALL SAY,*
WHAT HAVE I TO DO ANY MORE WITH IDOLS?
I HAVE HEARD *HIM,*
AND OBSERVED HIM:
I *AM* LIKE A GREEN FIR TREE.
FROM ME IS THY FRUIT FOUND.

I WILL BE AS THE DEW

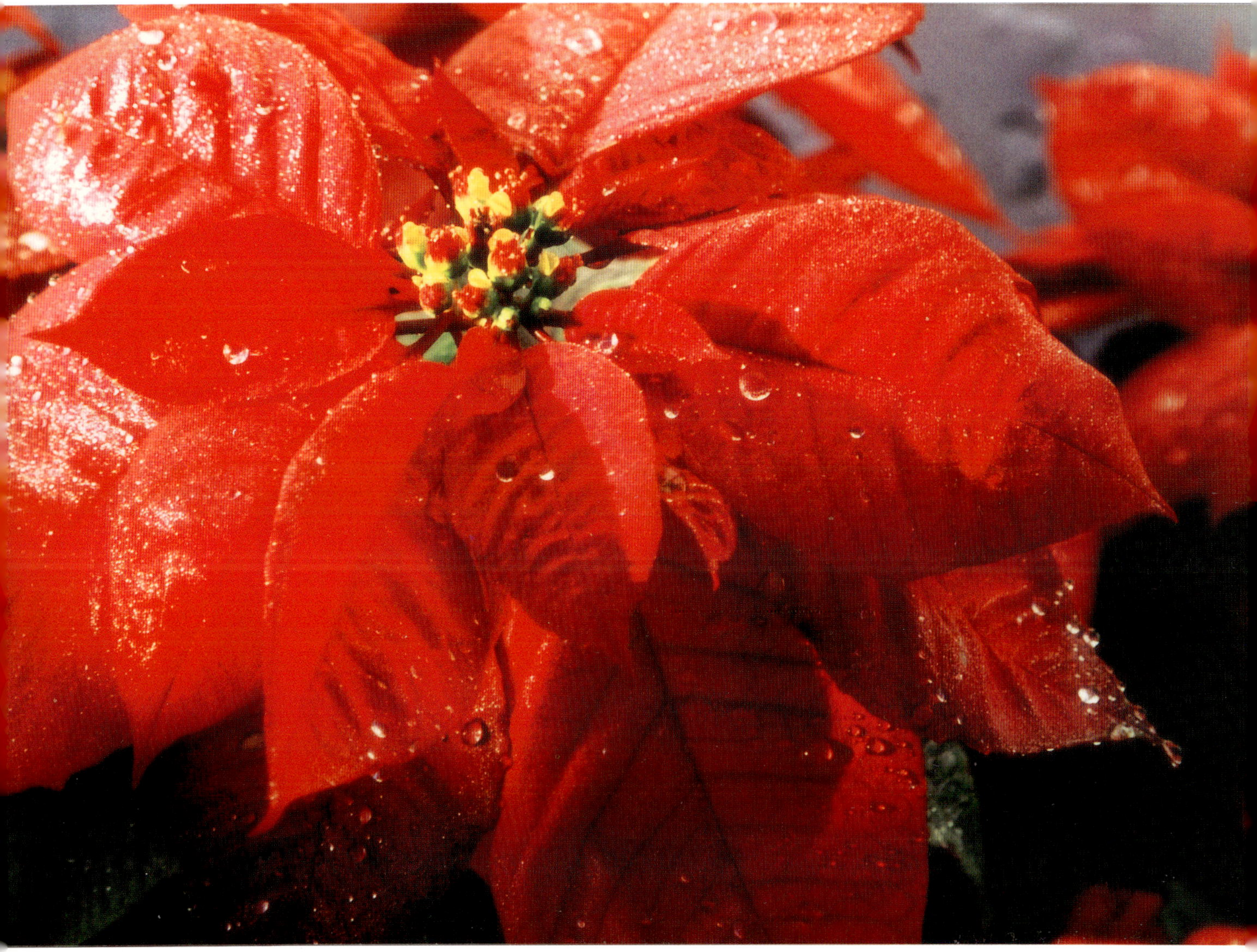

UNTO ISRAEL

Joel 2 : 25-29

AND I WILL RESTORE TO YOU THE YEARS THAT THE LOCUST HATH EATEN,
THE CANKERWORM, AND THE CATERPILLER, AND THE PALMERWORM,
MY GREAT ARMY WHICH I SENT AMONG YOU.

AND YE SHALL EAT IN PLENTY,
AND BE SATISFIED,
AND PRAISE THE NAME OF THE LORD YOUR GOD,
THAT HATH DEALT WONDROUSLY WITH YOU:
AND MY PEOPLE SHALL NEVER BE ASHAMED.

AND YE SHALL KNOW THAT I *AM* IN THE MIDST OF ISRAEL,
AND *THAT* I *AM* THE LORD YOUR GOD,
AND NONE ELSE:
AND MY PEOPLE SHALL NEVER BE ASHAMED.

AND IT SHALL COME TO PASS AFTERWARD,
THAT I WILL POUR OUT MY SPIRIT UPON ALL FLESH;
AND YOUR SONS AND YOUR DAUGHTERS SHALL PROPHESY,
YOUR OLD MEN SHALL DREAM DREAMS,
YOUR YOUNG MEN SHALL SEE VISIONS:

AND ALSO UPON THE SERVANTS AND UPON THE HANDMAIDS
IN THOSE DAYS WILL I POUR OUT MY SPIRIT.

AND I WILL RESTORE TO YOU THE YEARS THAT THE LOCUST HATH EATEN,

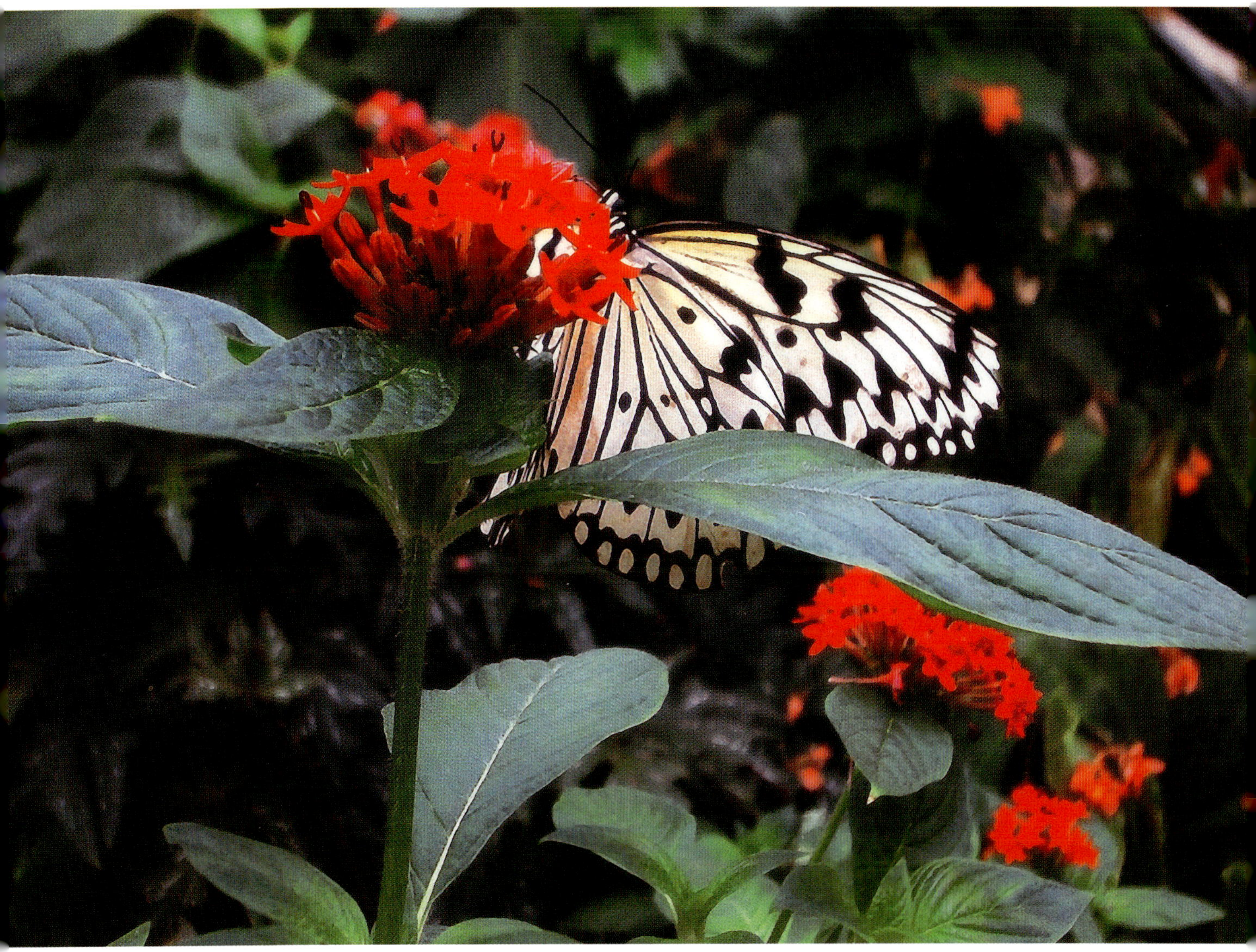

THE CANKERWORM, AND THE CATERPILLER

Amos 5 : 20-27

Shall not the day of the LORD *be* darkness, and not light?
even very dark, and no brightness in it?

I HATE, I DESPISE YOUR FEAST DAYS,
AND I WILL NOT SMELL IN YOUR SOLEMN ASSEMBLIES.

THOUGH YE OFFER ME BURNT OFFERINGS AND YOUR MEAT OFFERINGS,
I WILL NOT ACCEPT *THEM*:
NEITHER WILL I REGARD THE PEACE OFFERINGS OF YOUR FAT BEASTS.

TAKE THOU AWAY FROM ME THE NOISE OF THY SONGS;
FOR I WILL NOT HEAR THE MELODY OF THY VIOLS.

BUT LET JUDGEMENT RUN DOWN AS WATERS,
AND RIGHTEOUSNESS AS A MIGHTY STREAM.

HAVE YE OFFERED UNTO ME SACRIFICES AND OFFERINGS
IN THE WILDERNESS FORTY YEARS, O HOUSE OF ISRAEL?

BUT YE HAVE BORNE THE TABERNACLE OF YOUR MOLOCH AND CHIUN
YOUR IMAGES, THE STAR OF YOUR GOD, WHICH YE MADE TO YOURSELVES.

THEREFORE WILL I CAUSE YOU TO GO INTO CAPTIVITY BEYOND DAMASCUS,
saith the LORD, whose name *is* The God of hosts.

BUT LET JUDGEMENT RUN DOWN

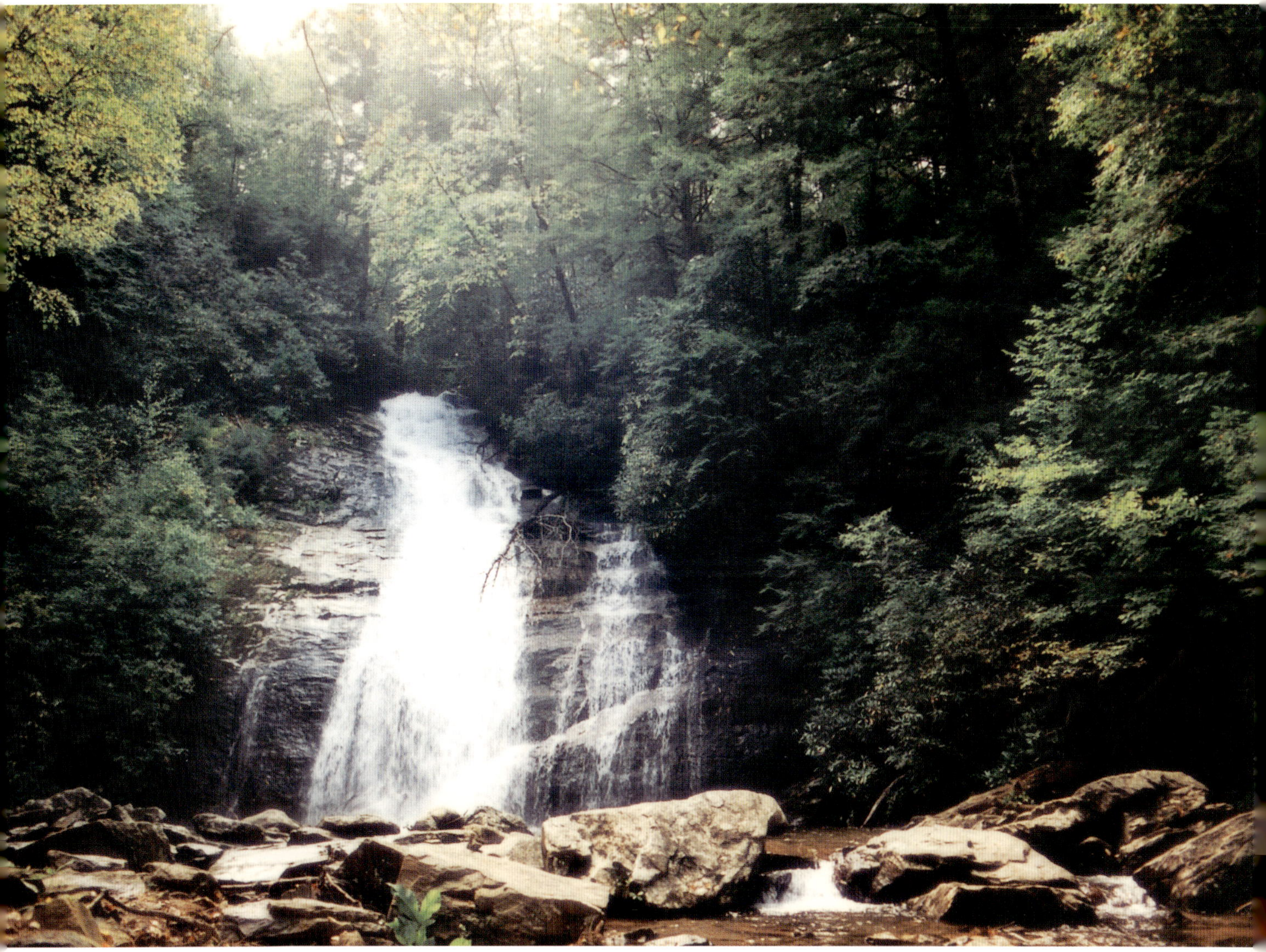

AS WATERS

FOR AS YE HAVE DRUNK UPON MY HOLY MOUNTAIN,
SO SHALL ALL THE HEATHEN DRINK CONTINUALLY,
YEA, THEY SHALL DRINK,
AND THEY SHALL SWALLOW DOWN,
AND THEY SHALL BE AS THOUGH THEY HAD NOT BEEN.

BUT UPON MOUNT ZION SHALL BE DELIVERANCE,
AND THERE SHALL BE HOLINESS;
AND THE HOUSE OF JACOB SHALL POSSESS THEIR POSSESSIONS.

AND THE HOUSE OF JACOB SHALL BE A FIRE,
AND THE HOUSE OF JOSEPH A FLAME,
AND THE HOUSE OF ESAU FOR STUBBLE,
AND THEY SHALL KINDLE IN THEM,
AND DEVOUR THEM;
AND THERE SHALL NOT BE *ANY* REMAINING OF THE HOUSE OF ESAU;
for the LORD hath spoken *it*.

And *they* of the south shall possess the mount of Esau;
and *they of* the plain the Philistines:
and they shall possess the fields of Ephraim,
and the fields of Samaria:
and Benjamin *shall possess* Gilead.

And *they* of the south

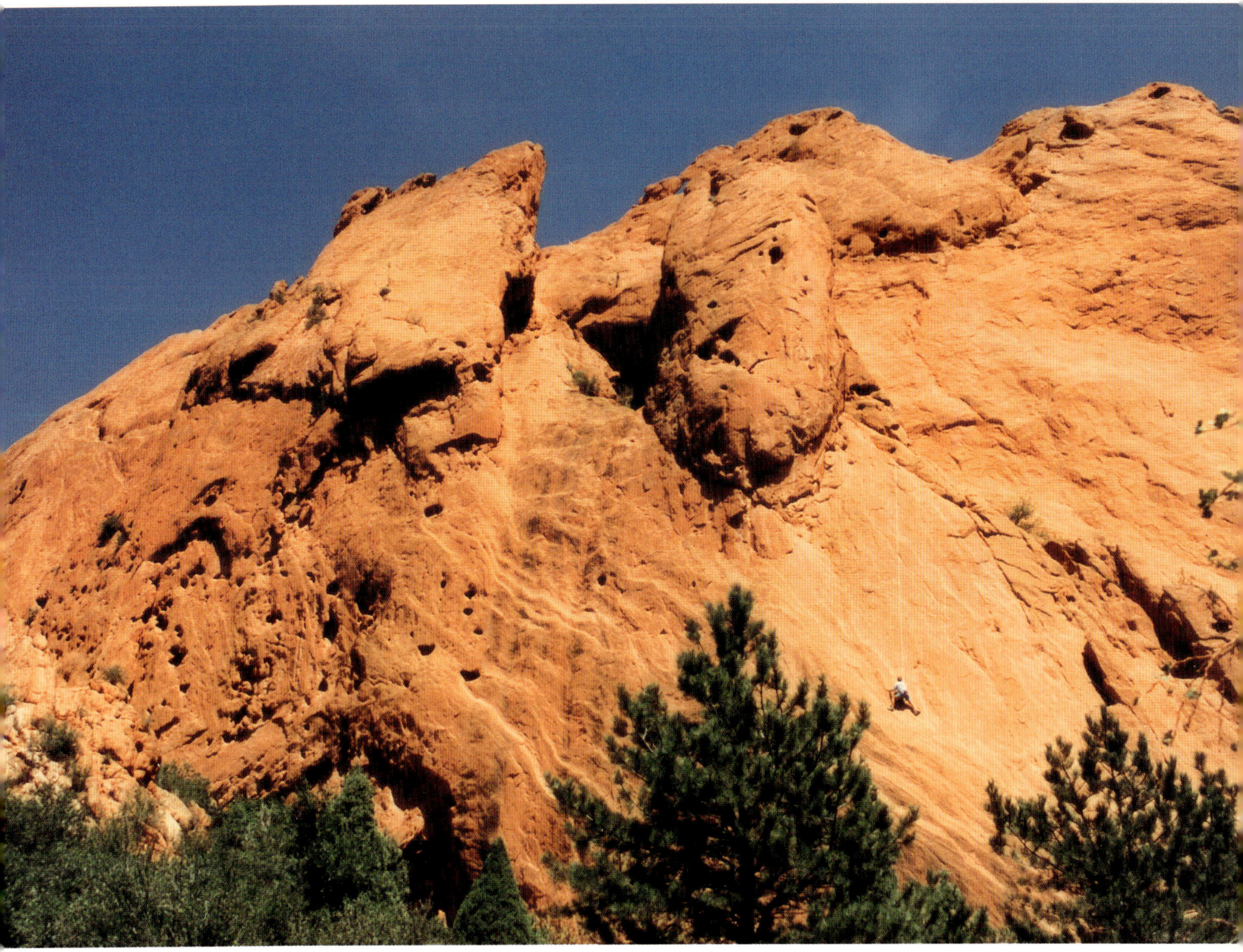

shall possess the mount of Esau

Jonah 1 : 17 - 2 : 1-7

Now the LORD had prepared a great fish to swallow up Jonah.
And Jonah was in the belly of the fish three days and three nights.

Then Jonah prayed unto the LORD his God out of the fish's belly,

And said, I cried by reason of mine affliction unto the LORD,
and he heard me; out of the belly of hell cried I,
and thou heardest my voice.

For thou hadst cast me into the deep, in the midst of the seas;
and the floods compassed me about:
all thy billows and thy waves passed over me.

Then I said, I am cast out of thy sight;
yet I will look again toward thy holy temple.

The water compassed me about, *even* to the soul:
the depth closed me round about,
the weeds were wrapped about my head.

I went down to the bottoms of the mountains;
the earth with her bars *was* about me for ever:
yet hast thou brought up my life from corruption, O LORD my God.

When my soul fainted within me I remembered the LORD:
and my prayer came in unto thee, into thine holy temple.

For thou hadst cast me into the deep,

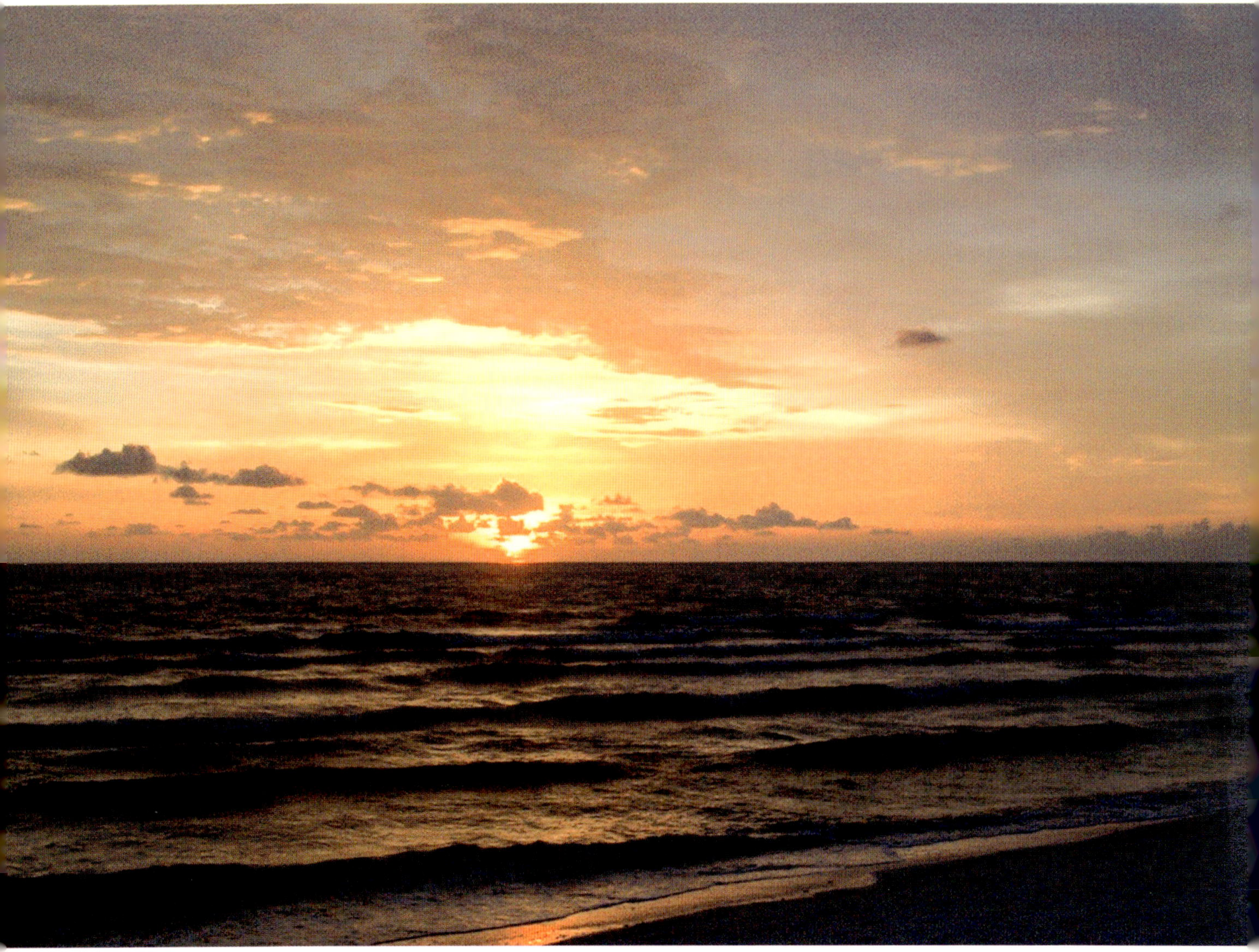

in the midst of the seas

Micah 7 : 18-20

Who *is* a God like unto thee,
that pardoneth iniquity,
and passeth by the transgression of the remnant of his heritage?
he retaineth not his anger for ever,
because he delighteth *in* mercy.

He will turn again,
he will have compassion upon us;
he will subdue our iniquities;
and thou wilt cast all their sins into the depths of the sea.

Thou wilt perform the truth to Jacob,
and the mercy to Abraham,
which thou hast sworn unto our fathers from the days of old.

and thou wilt cast all their sins

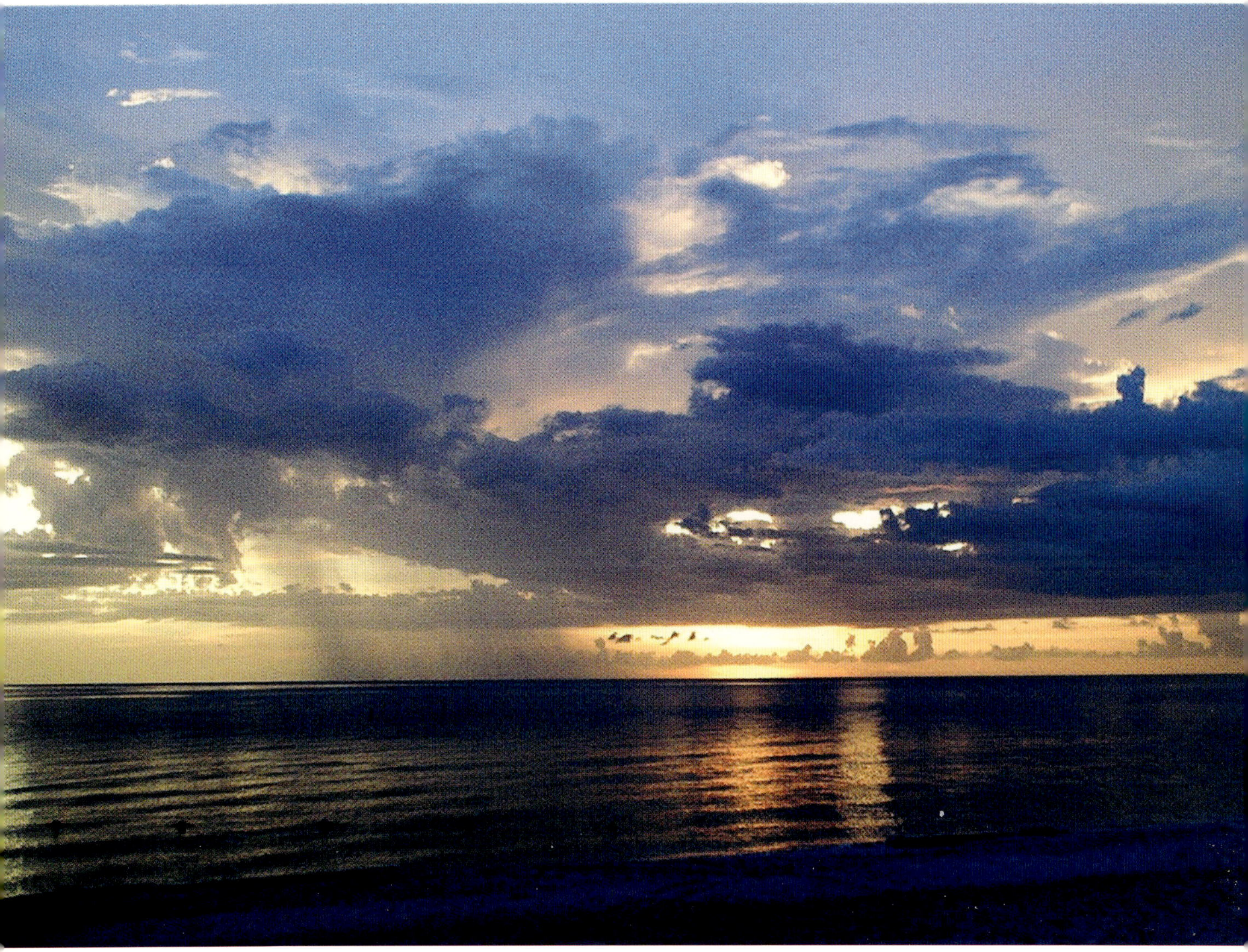

into the depths of the sea

Nahum 1 : 1-4

The burden of Nineveh.
The book of the vision of Nahum the Elkoshite.

God *is* jealous,
and the LORD revengeth;
the LORD revengeth,
and is furious;
the LORD will take vengeance on his adversaries,
and he reserveth *wrath* for his enemies.

The LORD *is* slow to anger,
and great in power,
and will not at all acquit *the wicked:*
the LORD *hath* his way in the whirlwind and in the storm,
and the clouds *are* the dust of his feet.

He rebuketh the sea,
and maketh it dry,
and drieth up all the rivers;
Bashan languisheth,
and Carmel,
and the flower of Lebanon languisheth.

the LORD *hath* his way in the whirlwind and in the storm,

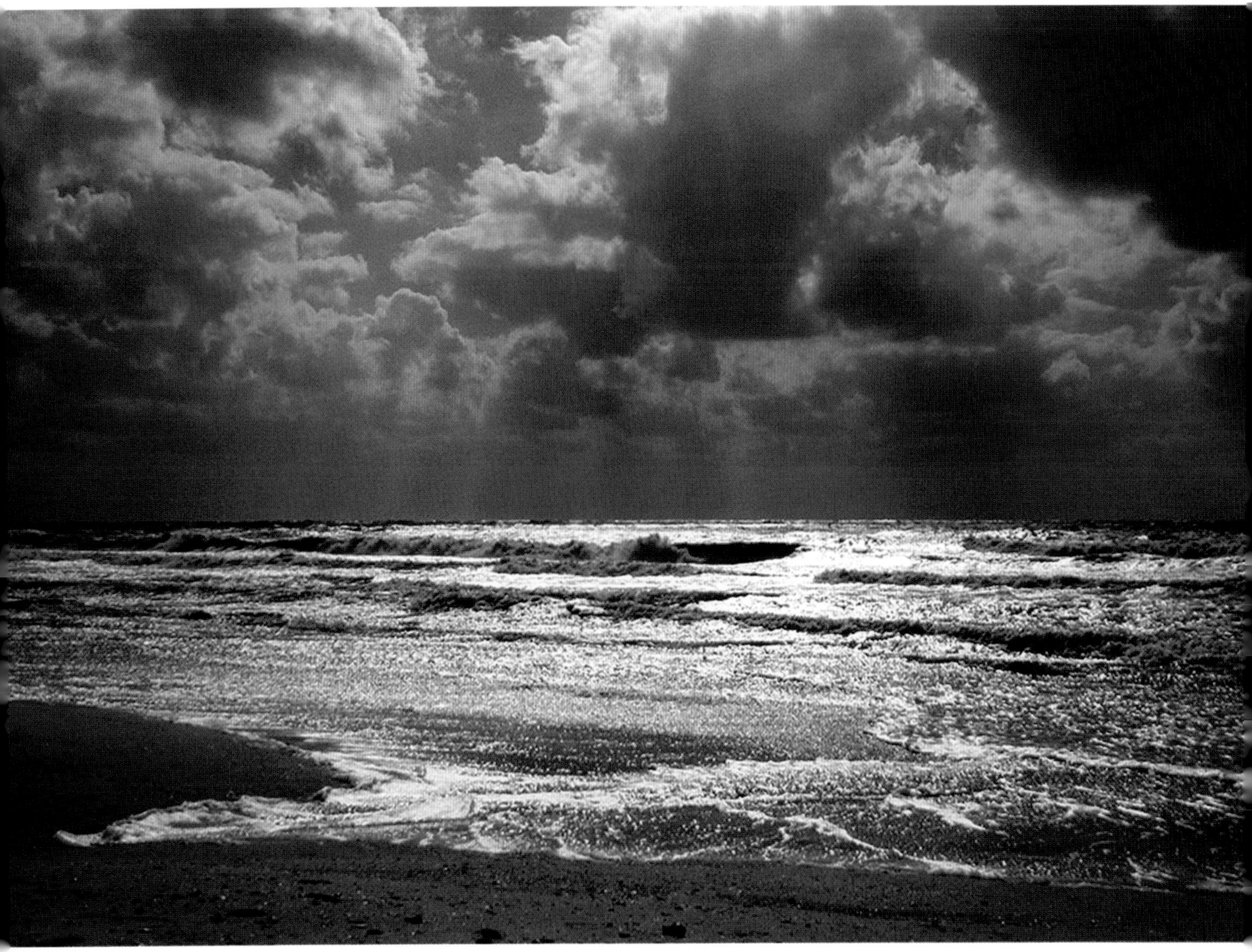

and the clouds *are* the dust of his feet

Habakkuk 2 : 1-4

I will stand upon my watch,
and set me upon the tower,
and will watch to see what he will say unto me,
and what I shall answer when I am reproved.

And the LORD answered me,
and said,
WRITE THE VISION,
AND MAKE *IT* PLAIN UPON TABLES,
THAT HE MAY RUN THAT READETH IT.

FOR THE VISION *IS* YET FOR AN APPOINTED TIME,
BUT AT THE END IT SHALL SPEAK,
AND NOT LIE:
THOUGH IT TARRY,
WAIT FOR IT;
BECAUSE IT WILL SURELY COME,
IT WILL NOT TARRY.

BEHOLD,
HIS SOUL *WHICH* IS LIFTED UP IS NOT UPRIGHT IN HIM:
BUT THE JUST SHALL LIVE BY HIS FAITH.

THOUGH IT TARRY,

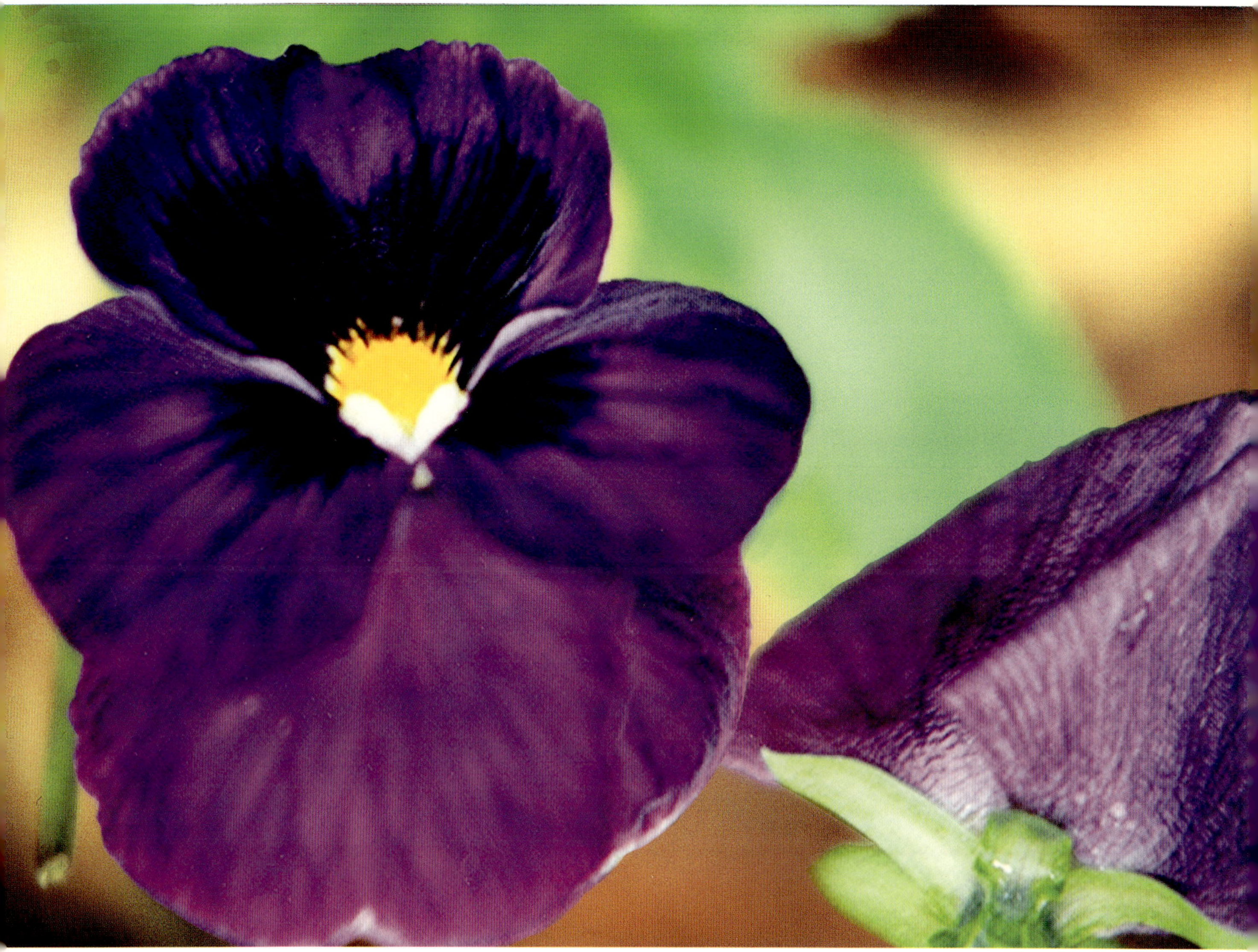

WAIT FOR IT

Zephaniah 1 : 2-6

I WILL UTTERLY CONSUME ALL *THINGS* FROM OFF THE LAND,
saith the LORD.

I WILL CONSUME MAN AND BEAST;
I WILL CONSUME THE FOWLS OF THE HEAVEN,
AND THE FISHES OF THE SEA,
AND THE STUMBLINGBLOCKS WITH THE WICKED;
AND I WILL CUT OFF MAN FROM OFF THE LAND,
saith the LORD.

I WILL ALSO STRETCH OUT MINE HAND UPON JUDAH,
AND UPON ALL THE INHABITANTS OF JERUSALEM;
AND I WILL CUT OFF THE REMNANT OF BAAL FROM THIS PLACE,
AND THE NAME OF THE CHEMARIMS WITH THE PRIESTS;

AND THEM THAT WORSHIP THE HOST OF HEAVEN UPON THE HOUSETOPS;
AND THEM THAT WORSHIP *AND* THAT SWEAR BY THE LORD,
AND THAT SWEAR BY MALCHAM;

AND THEM THAT ARE TURNED BACK FROM THE LORD;
AND *THOSE* THAT HAVE NOT SOUGHT THE LORD,
NOR ENQUIRED FOR HIM.

I WILL UTTERLY CONSUME ALL *THINGS* FROM OFF THE LAND,

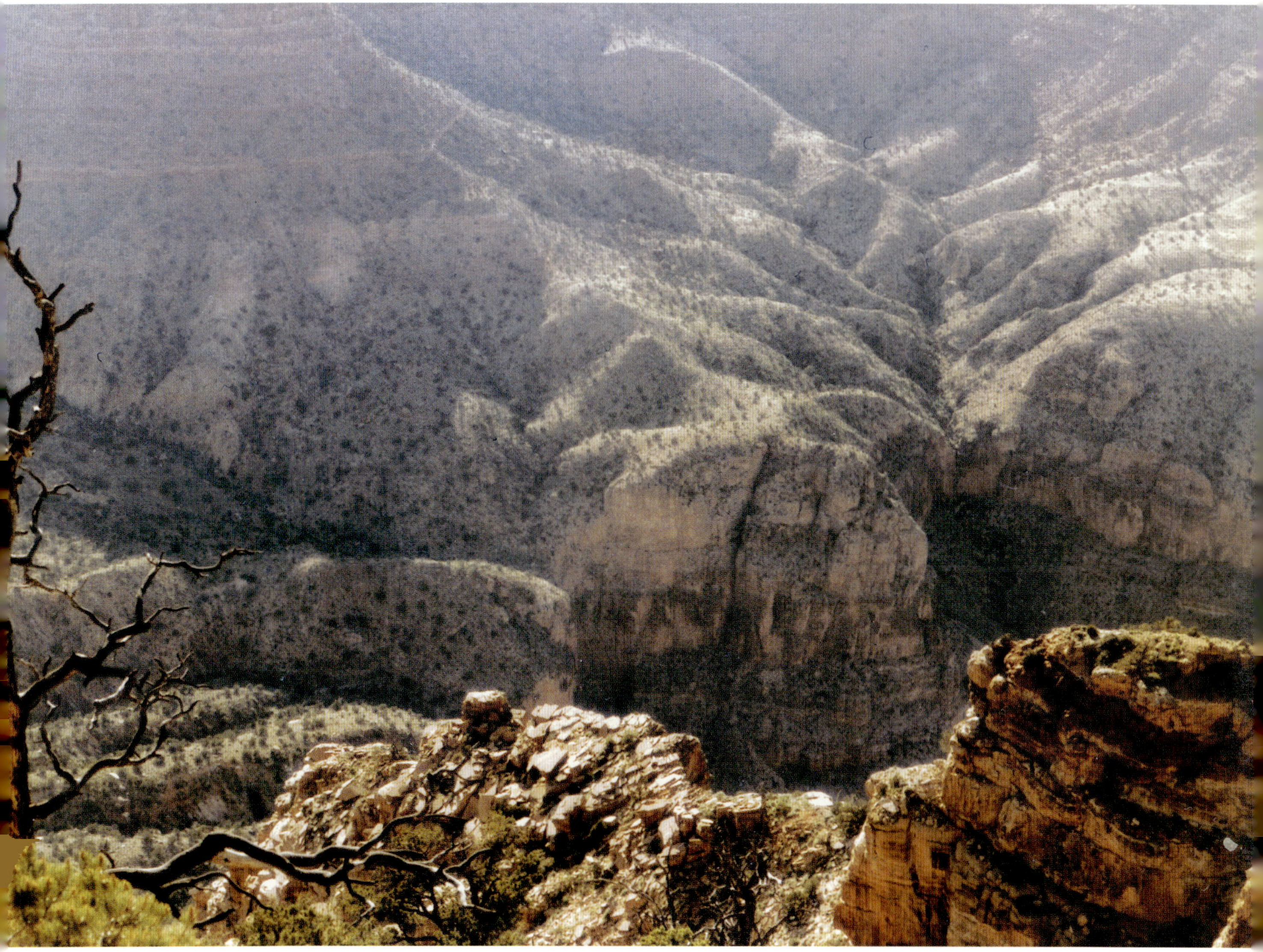

saith the LORD

AND I CALLED FOR A DROUGHT UPON THE LAND,
AND UPON THE MOUNTAINS,
AND UPON THE CORN,
AND UPON THE NEW WINE,
AND UPON THE OIL,
AND UPON *THAT* WHICH THE GROUND BRINGETH FORTH,
AND UPON MEN,
AND UPON CATTLE,
AND UPON ALL THE LABOUR OF THE HANDS.

Then Zerubbabel the son of Shealtiel,
and Joshua the son of Josedech, the high priest,
with all the remnant of the people,
obeyed the voice of the LORD their God,
and the words of Haggai the prophet,
as the LORD their God had sent him,
and the people did fear before the LORD.

Then spake Haggai the LORD'S messenger
in the LORD'S message unto the people saying,
I *AM* WITH YOU,
saith the LORD.

AND I CALLED FOR A DROUGHT UPON THE LAND,

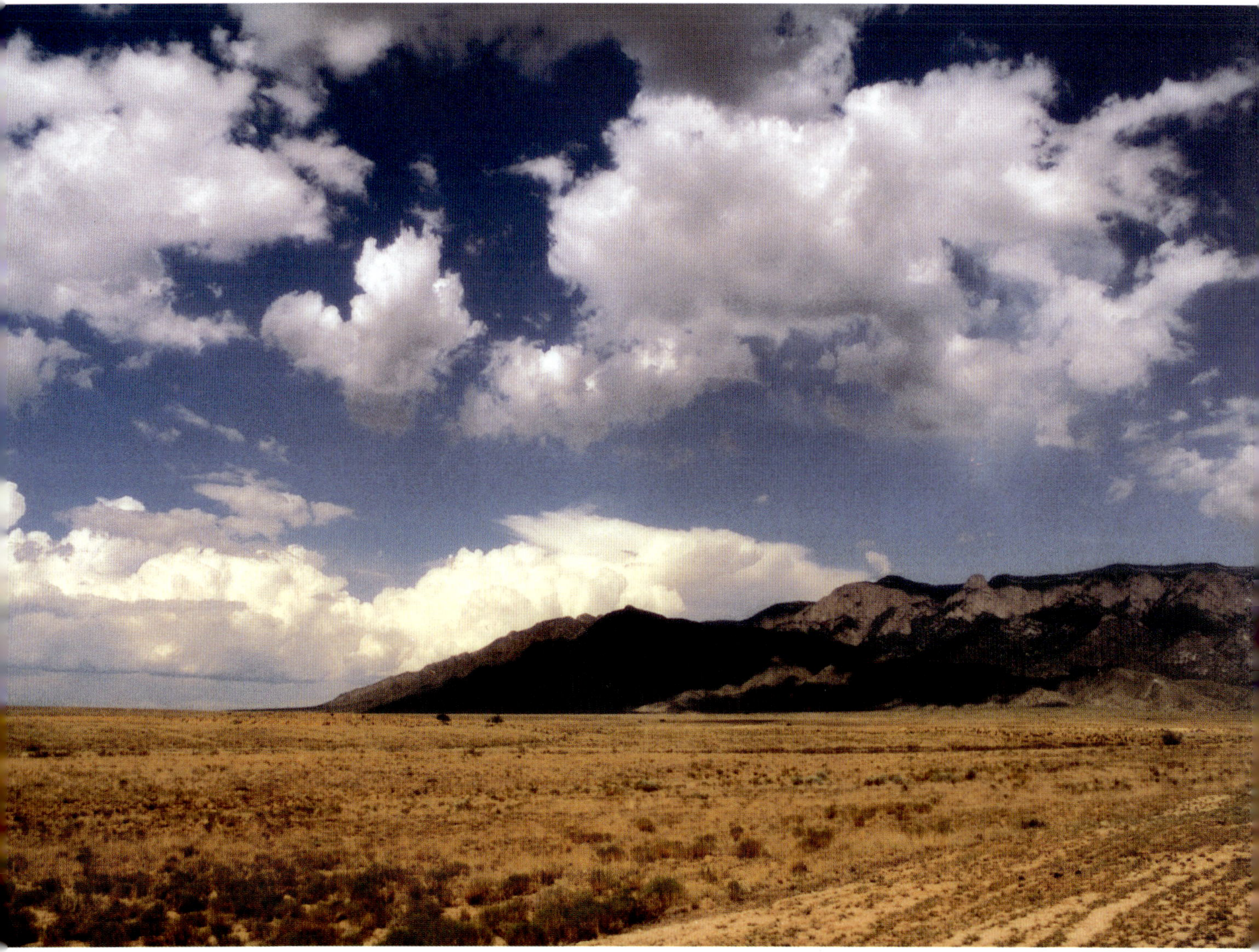

AND UPON MOUNTAINS

Zechariah 3 : 6-10

And the angel of the LORD protested unto Joshua, saying,

Thus saith the LORD of hosts;
IF THOU WILT WALK IN MY WAYS,
AND IF THOU WILT KEEP MY CHARGE,
THEN THOU SHALT ALSO JUDGE MY HOUSE,
AND SHALT ALSO KEEP MY COURTS,
AND I WILL GIVE THEE PLACES TO WALK AMONG THESE THAT STAND BY.

HEAR NOW, O JOSHUA THE HIGH PRIEST,
THOU, AND THY FELLOWS THAT SIT BEFORE THEE:
FOR THEY *ARE* MEN WONDERED AT:
FOR, BEHOLD,
I WILL BRING FORTH MY SERVANT THE BRANCH.

FOR BEHOLD THE STONE THAT I HAVE LAID BEFORE JOSHUA;
UPON ONE STONE *SHALL BE* SEVEN EYES:
BEHOLD, I WILL ENGRAVE THE GRAVING THEREOF,
saith the LORD of hosts,
AND I WILL REMOVE THE INIQUITY OF THAT LAND IN ONE DAY.

IN THAT DAY,
saith the LORD of hosts,
SHALL YE CALL EVERY MAN HIS NEIGHBOUR
UNDER THE VINE AND UNDER THE FIG TREE.

I WILL BRING FORTH MY SERVANT

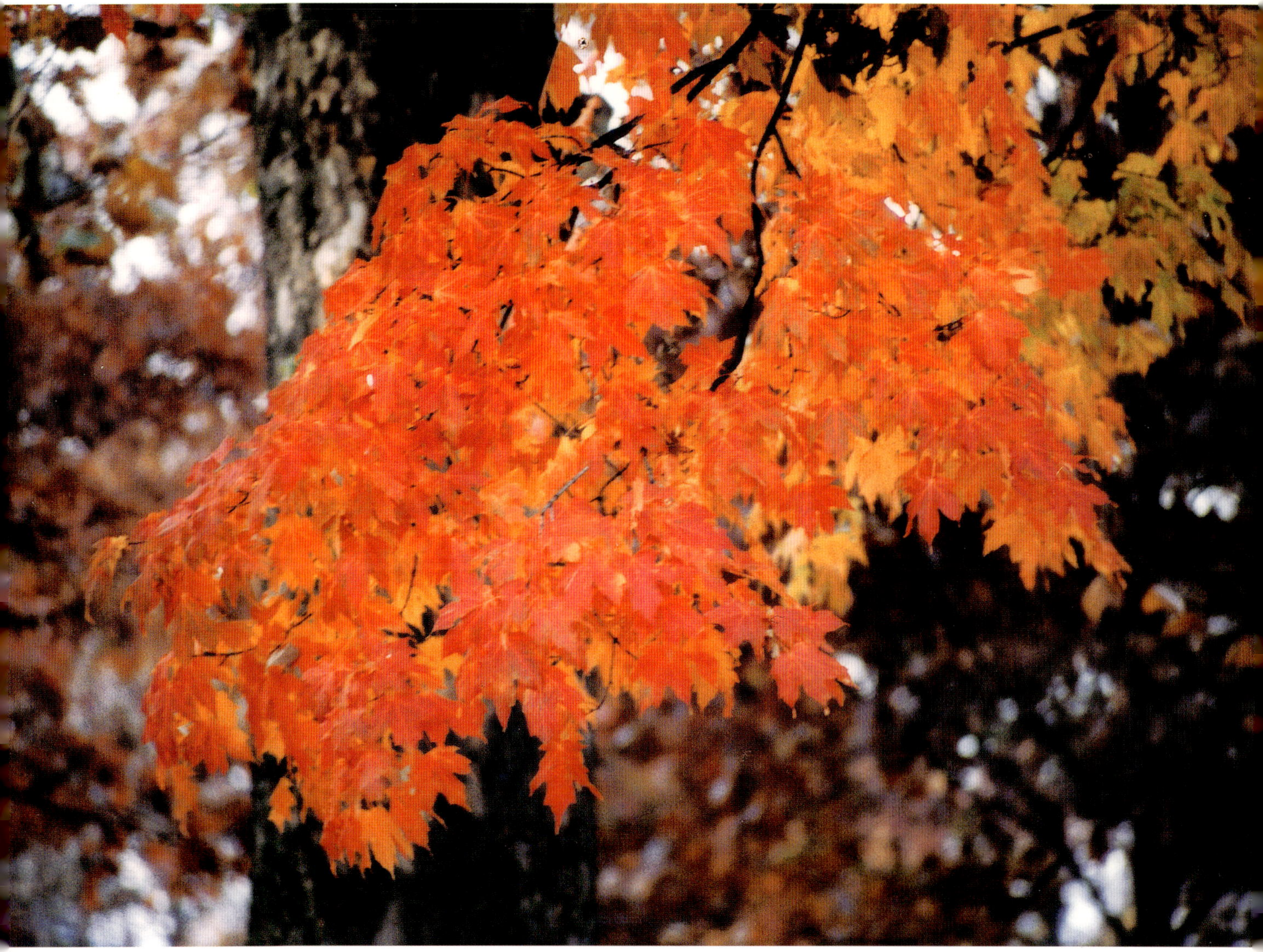

THE BRANCH

Malachi 1 : 11-13

FOR FROM THE RISING OF THE SUN
EVEN UNTO THE GOING DOWN OF THE SAME
MY NAME *SHALL BE* GREAT AMONG THE GENTILES;
AND IN EVERY PLACE INCENSE *SHALL BE* OFFERED UNTO MY NAME,
AND A PURE OFFERING:
FOR MY NAME *SHALL BE* GREAT AMONG THE HEATHEN,
saith the LORD of hosts.

BUT YE HAVE PROFANED IT,
IN THAT YE SAY,
THE TABLE OF THE LORD *IS* POLLUTED;
AND THE FRUIT THEREOF, *EVEN* HIS MEAT,
IS CONTEMPTIBLE.

YE SAID ALSO,
BEHOLD, WHAT A WEARINESS *IS IT!*
AND YE HAVE SNUFFED AT IT,
saith the LORD of hosts;
AND YE BROUGHT *THAT WHICH WAS* TORN,
AND THE LAME, AND THE SICK;
THUS YE BROUGHT AN OFFERING:
SHOULD I ACCEPT THIS OF YOUR HAND?
saith the LORD.

FOR FROM THE RISING OF THE SUN

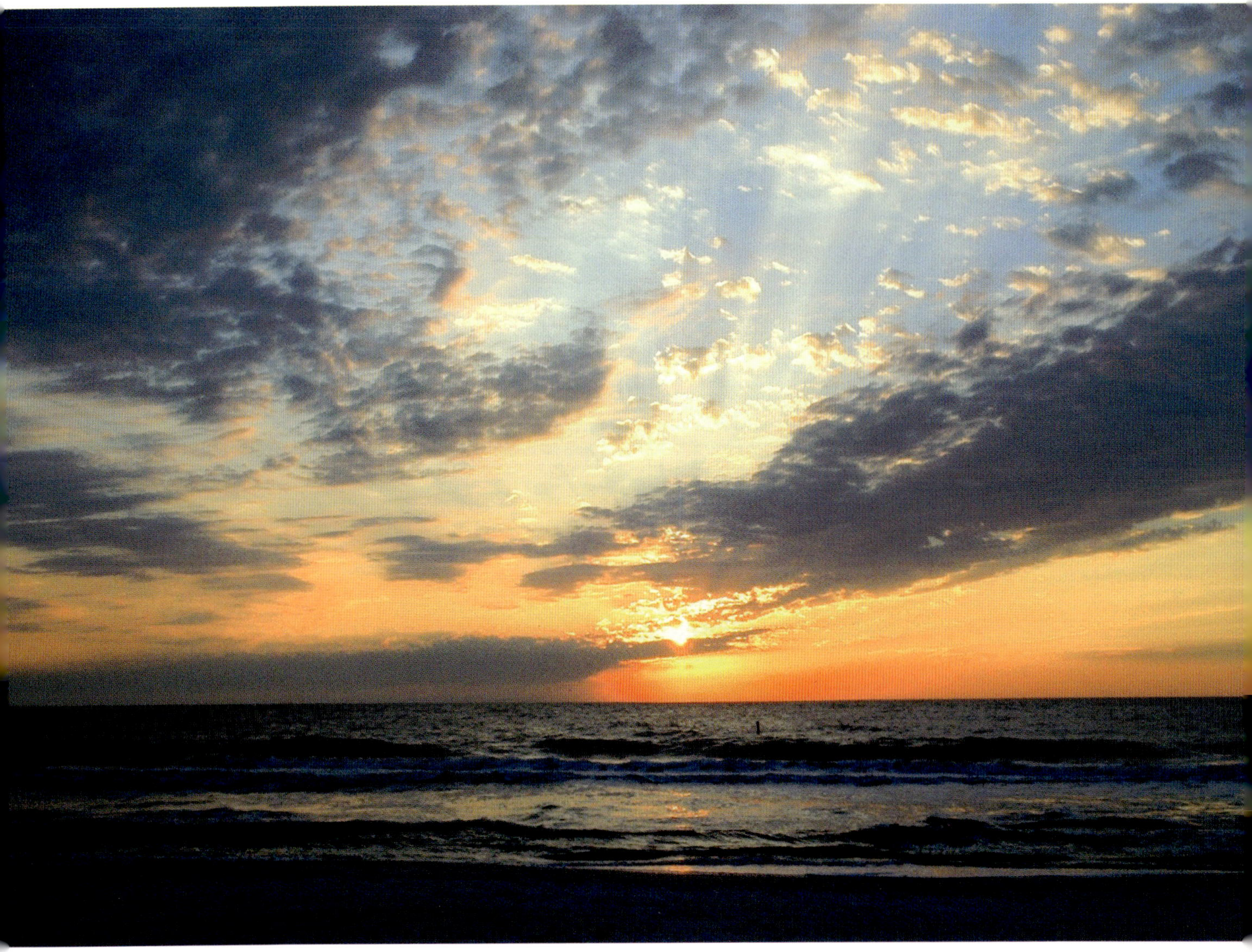

EVEN UNTO THE GOING DOWN OF THE SAME

Matthew 16 : 1-4

The Pharisees also with the Sadducees came,
and tempting desired him that he would shew them a sign from heaven.

He answered and said unto them,
WHEN IT IS EVENING,
YE SAY,
IT WILL BE FAIR WEATHER:
FOR THE SKY IS RED.

AND IN THE MORNING,
IT WILL BE FOUL WEATHER TO DAY:
FOR THE SKY IS RED A LOWRING.
O *YE* HYPOCRITES,
YE CAN DISCERN THE FACE OF THE SKY;
BUT CAN YE NOT *DISCERN* THE SIGNS OF THE TIMES?

A WICKED AND ADULTEROUS GENERATION SEEKETH AFTER A SIGN;
AND THERE SHALL NO SIGN BE GIVEN UNTO IT,
BUT THE SIGN OF THE PROPHET JONAS.
And he left them, and departed.

IT WILL BE FOUL WEATHER TO DAY:

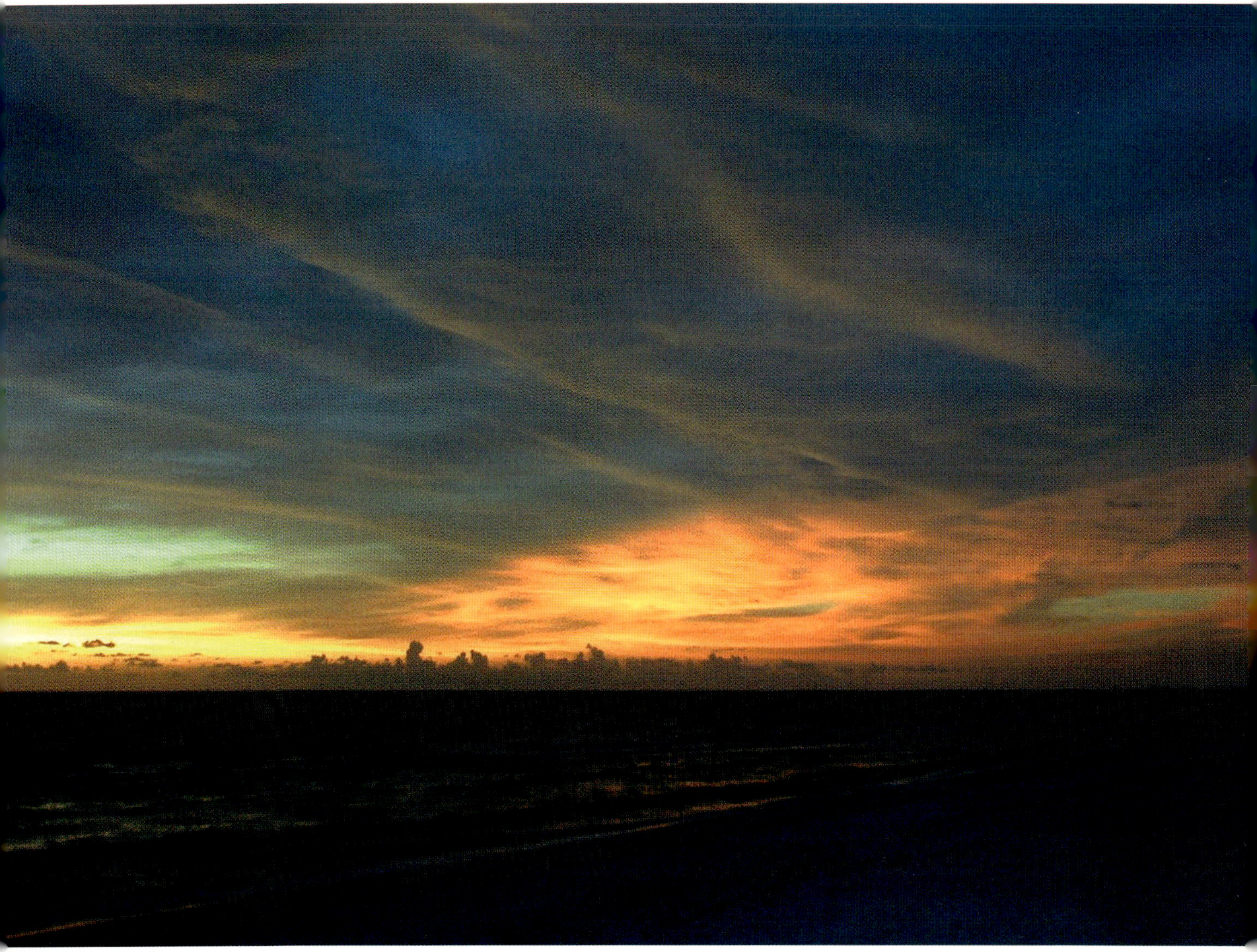

FOR THE SKY IS RED AND LOWRING

Mark 4 : 37-41

And there arose a great storm of wind,
and the waves beat into the ship,
so that it was now full.

And he was in the hinder part of the ship, asleep on a pillow:
and they awake him, and say unto him,
Master, carest thou not that we perish?

And he arose, and rebuked the wind,
and said unto the sea,
PEACE, BE STILL.
And the wind ceased,
and there was a great calm.

And he said unto them,
WHY ARE YE SO FEARFUL?
HOW IS IT THAT YE HAVE NO FAITH?

And they feared exceedingly,
and said one to another,
What manner of man is this,
that even the wind and the sea obey him?

And
the
wind
ceased,

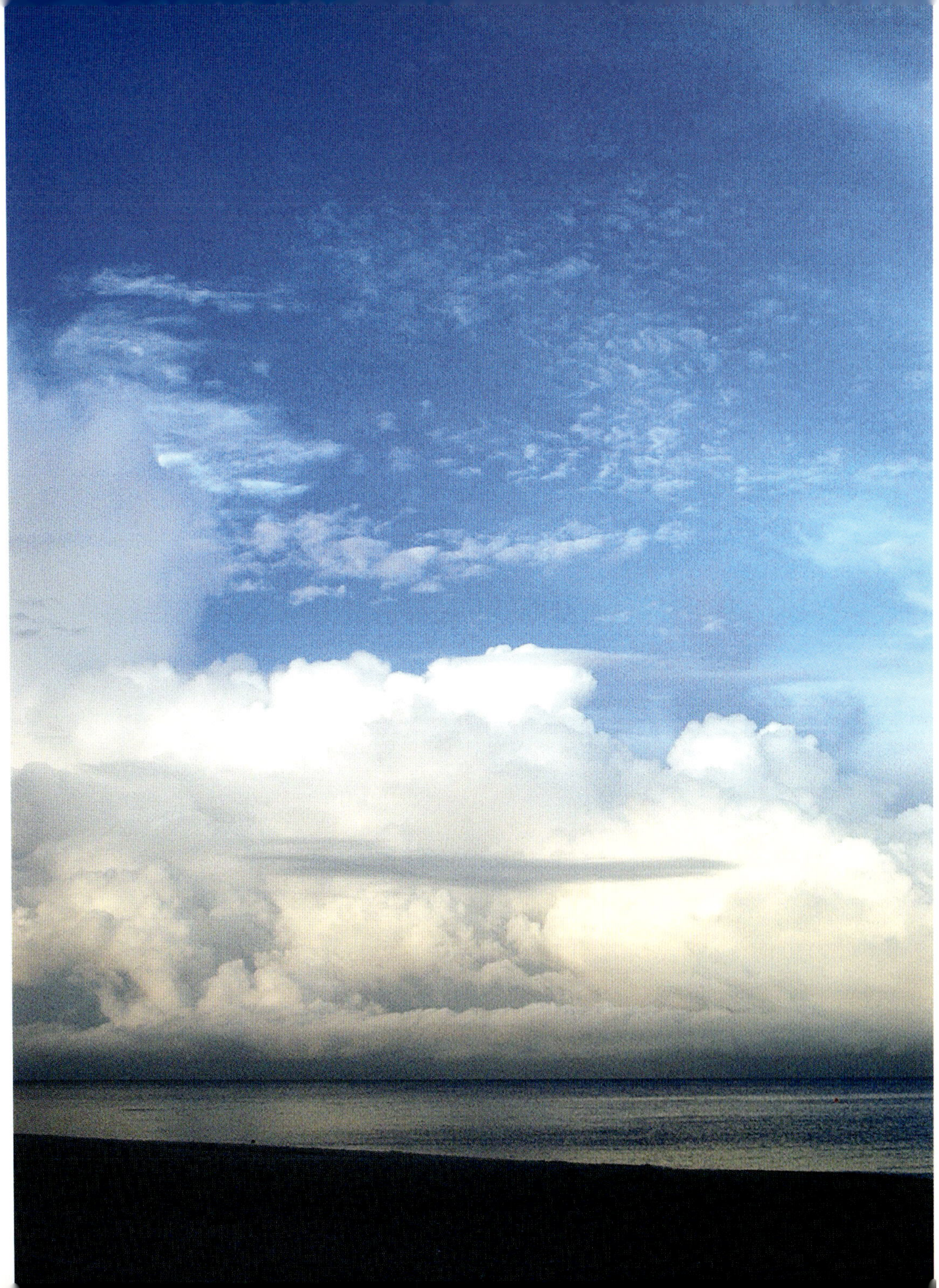

and
there
was
a
great
calm

Luke 8 : 11-15

NOW THE PARABLE IS THIS: THE SEED IS THE WORD OF GOD.

THOSE BY THE WAY SIDE ARE THEY THAT HEAR;
THEN COMETH THE DEVIL,
AND TAKETH AWAY THE WORD OUT OF THEIR HEARTS,
LEST THEY SHOULD BELIEVE AND BE SAVED.

THEY ON THE ROCK *ARE THEY*, WHICH,
WHEN THEY HEAR,
RECEIVE THE WORD WITH JOY;
AND THESE HAVE NO ROOT,
WHICH FOR A WHILE BELIEVE,
AND IN TIME OF TEMPTATION FALL AWAY.

AND THAT WHICH FELL AMONG THORNS ARE THEY, WHICH
WHEN THEY HAVE HEARD, GO FORTH,
AND ARE CHOKED WITH CARES AND RICHES AND PLEASURES
OF *THIS* LIFE,
AND BRING NO FRUIT TO PERFECTION.

BUT THAT ON THE GOOD GROUND ARE THEY,
WHICH IN AN HONEST AND GOOD HEART,
HAVING HEARD THE WORD,
KEEP *IT*,
AND BRING FORTH FRUIT WITH PATIENCE.

AND BRING FORTH FRUIT

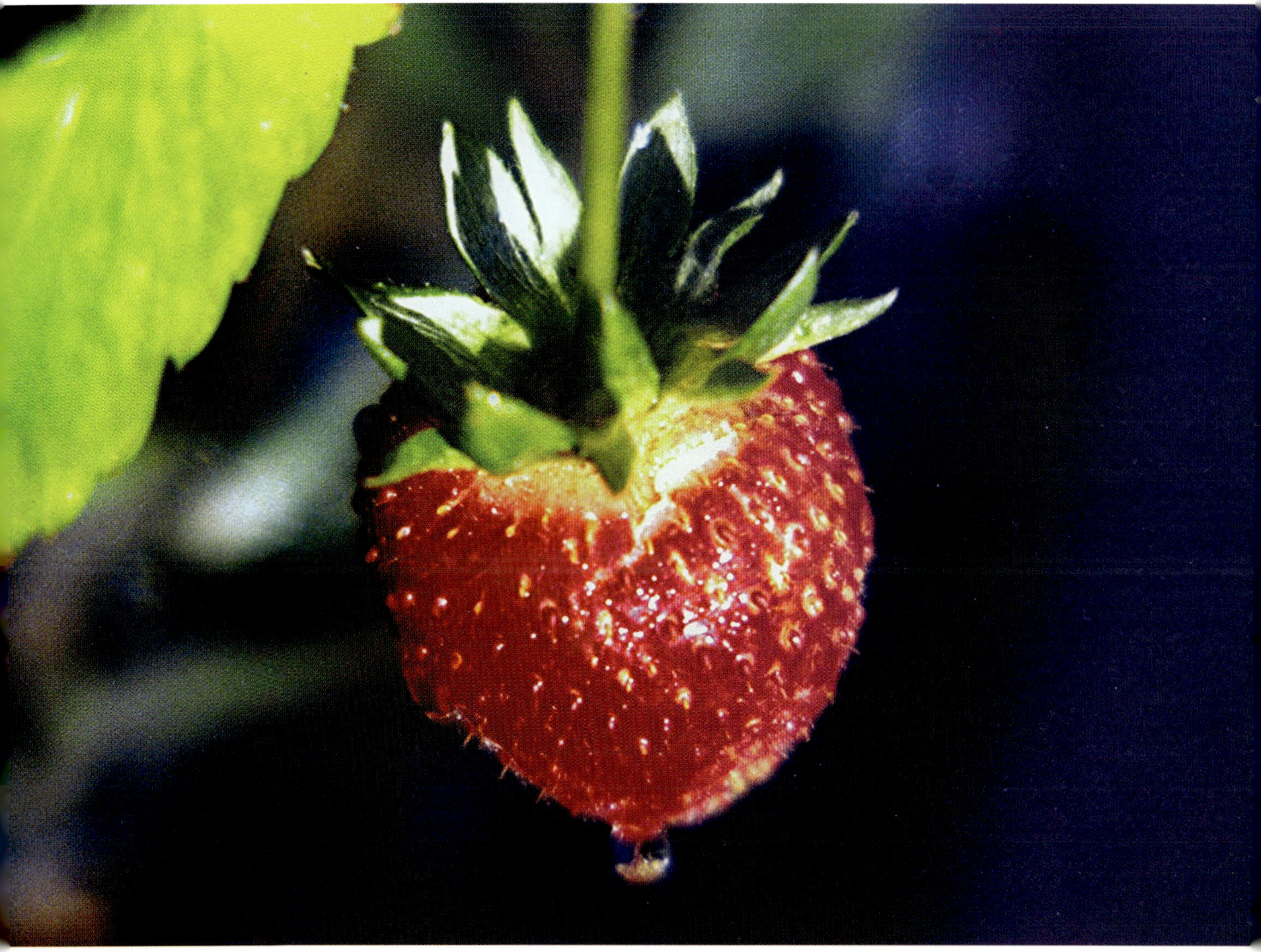

WITH PATIENCE

John 3 : 16-21

FOR GOD SO LOVED THE WORLD,
THAT HE GAVE HIS ONLY BEGOTTEN SON,
THAT WHOSOEVER BELIEVETH IN HIM SHOULD NOT PERISH,
BUT HAVE EVERLASTING LIFE.

FOR GOD SENT NOT HIS SON INTO THE WORLD TO CONDEMN THE WORLD;
BUT THAT THE WORLD THROUGH HIM MIGHT BE SAVED.

HE THAT BELIEVETH ON HIM IS NOT CONDEMNED:
BUT HE THAT BELIEVETH NOT IS CONDEMNED ALREADY,
BECAUSE HE HATH NOT BELIEVED IN THE NAME OF
THE ONLY BEGOTTEN SON OF GOD.

AND THIS IS THE CONDEMNATION,
THAT LIGHT IS COME INTO THE WORLD,
AND MEN LOVED DARKNESS RATHER THAN LIGHT,
BECAUSE THEIR DEEDS WERE EVIL.

FOR EVERY ONE THAT DOETH EVIL HATETH THE LIGHT,
NEITHER COMETH TO THE LIGHT,
LEST HIS DEEDS SHOULD BE REPROVED.

BUT HE THAT DOETH TRUTH COMETH TO THE LIGHT,
THAT HIS DEEDS MAY BE MADE MANIFEST,
THAT THEY ARE WROUGHT IN GOD.

AND MEN LOVED DARKNESS

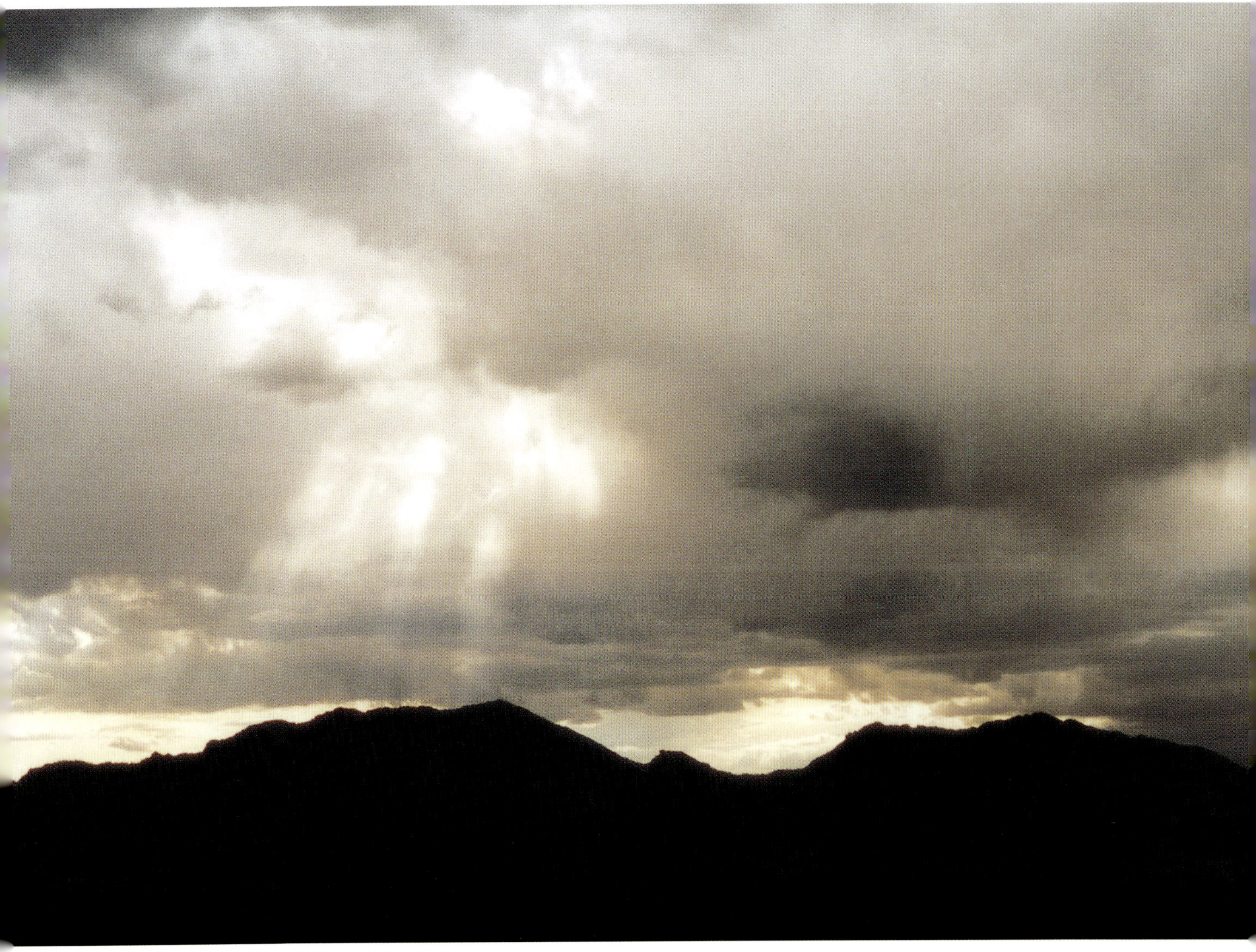

RATHER THAN LIGHT

Acts 26 : 13-18

At midday, O king, I saw in the way a light from heaven,
above the brightness of the sun,
shining round about me and them which journeyed with me.

And when we were all fallen to the earth,
I heard a voice speaking unto me, and saying in the Hebrew tongue,
SAUL, SAUL, WHY PERSECUTEST THOU ME?
IT IS HARD FOR THEE TO KICK AGAINST THE PRICKS.

And I said, Who art thou, Lord? And he said,
I AM JESUS WHOM THOU PERSECUTEST.

BUT RISE, AND STAND UPON THY FEET:
FOR I HAVE APPEARED UNTO THEE FOR THIS PURPOSE,
TO MAKE THEE A MINISTER AND A WITNESS
BOTH OF THESE THINGS WHICH THOU HAST SEEN,
AND OF THOSE THINGS IN THE WHICH I WILL APPEAR UNTO THEE;

DELIVERING THEE FROM THE PEOPLE,
AND *FROM* THE GENTILES, UNTO WHOM NOW I SEND THEE,

TO OPEN THEIR EYES, *AND* TO TURN *THEM* FROM DARKNESS TO LIGHT,
AND *FROM* THE POWER OF SATAN UNTO GOD,
THAT THEY MAY RECEIVE FORGIVENESS OF SINS,
AND INHERITANCE AMONG THEM WHICH ARE SANCTIFIED
BY FAITH THAT IS IN ME.

AND TO TURN *THEM* FROM DARKNESS

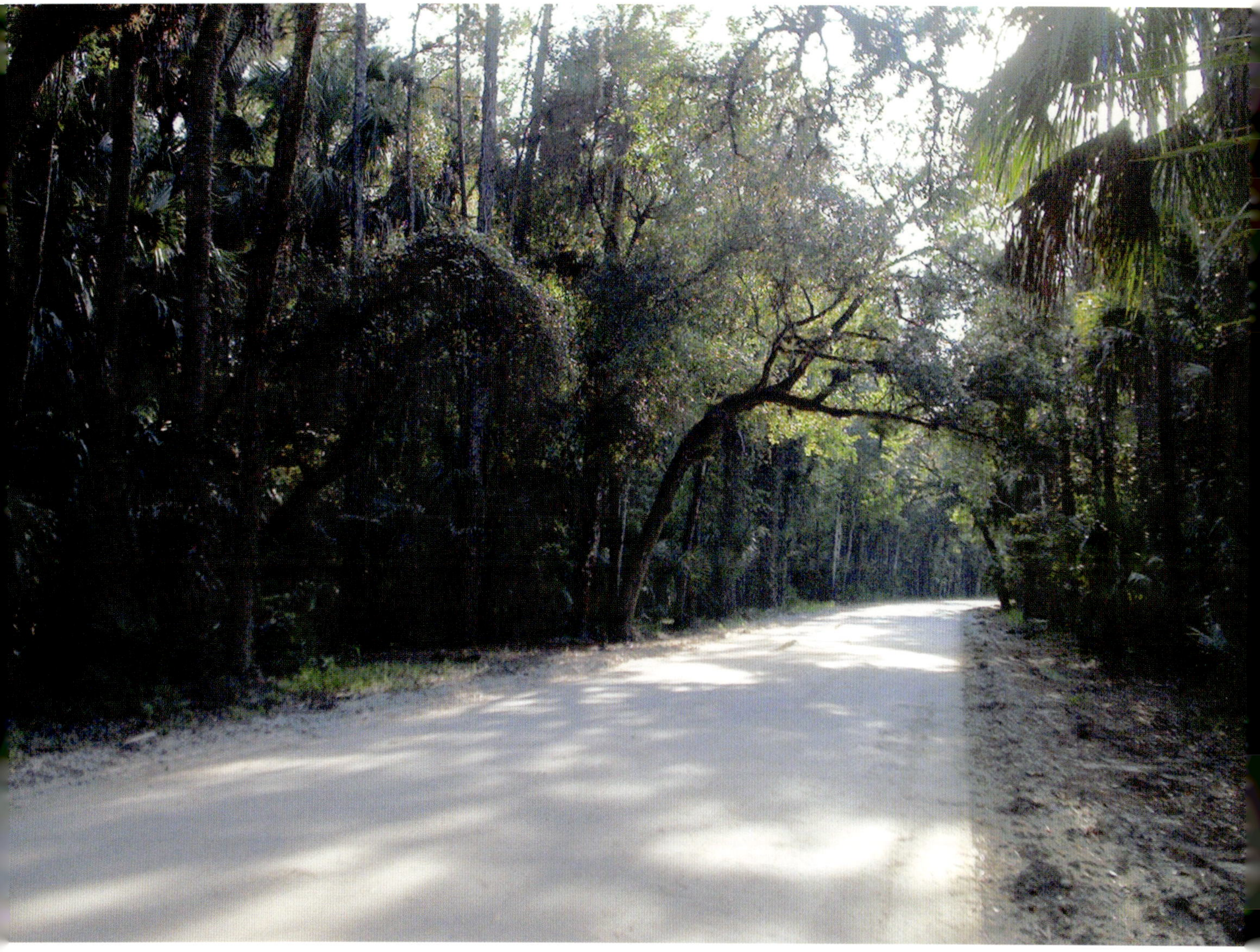

TO LIGHT

Romans 8 : 35-39

Who shall separate us from the love of Christ?
shall tribulation, or distress,
or persecution, or famine,
or nakedness, or peril, or sword?

As it is written,
For thy sake we are killed all the day long;
we are accounted as sheep for the slaughter.

Nay,
in all these things we are more than conquerors through him that loved us.

For I am persuaded,
that neither death, nor life,
nor angels,
nor principalities, nor powers,
nor things present,
nor things to come,

Nor height, nor depth,
nor any other creature,
shall be able to separate us from the love of God,
which is in Christ Jesus our Lord.

Nor
height,

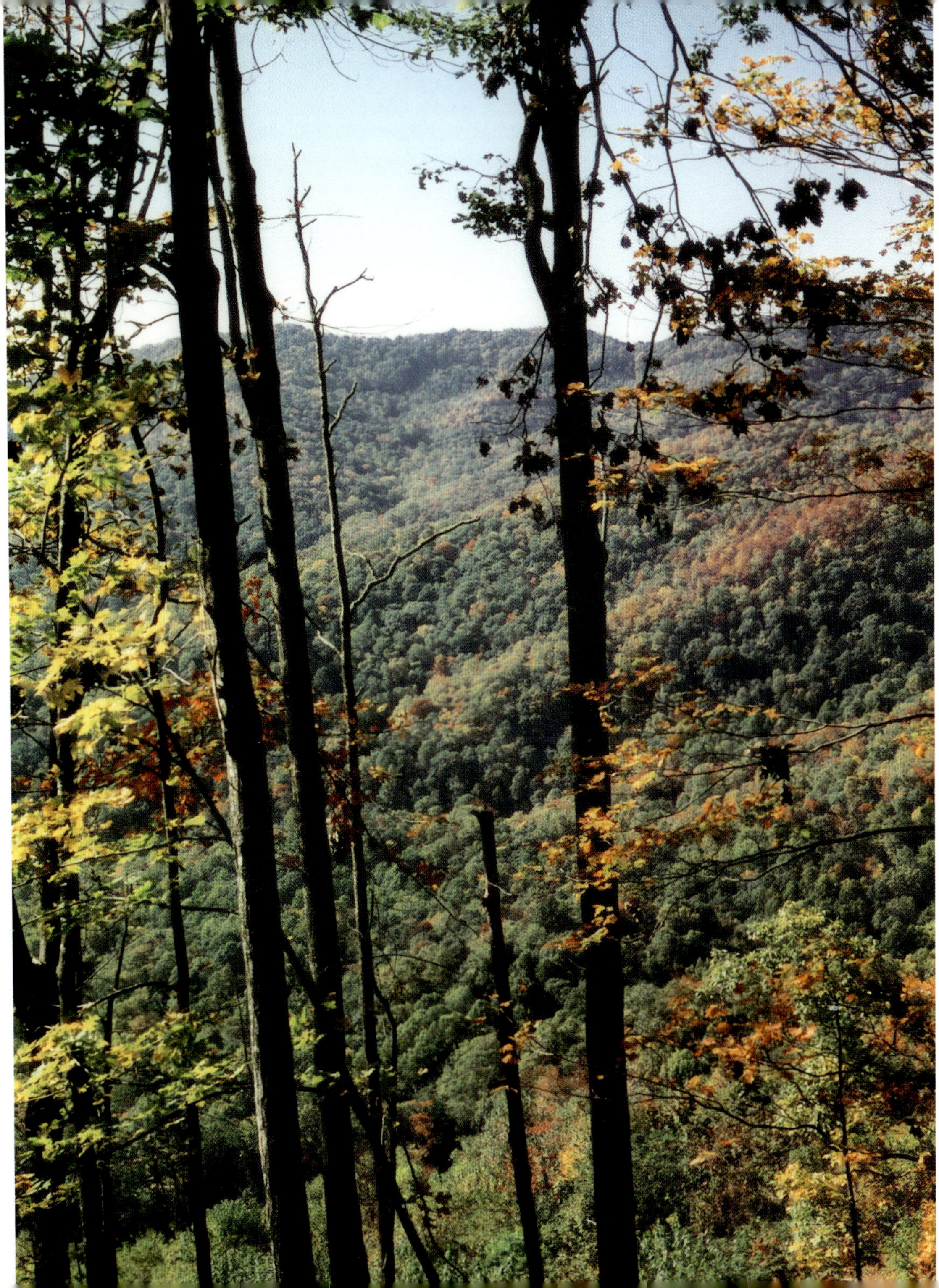

nor
depth

1 Corinthians 15 : 40-45

There are also celestial bodies,
and bodies terrestrial:
but the glory of the celestial *is* one,
and the *glory* of the terrestrial *is* another.

There is one glory of the sun,
and another glory of the moon,
and another glory of the stars:
for *one* star differeth from *another* star in glory.

So also *is* the resurrection of the dead.
It is sown in corruption; it is raised in incorruption:

It is sown in dishonour; it is raised in glory:
it is sown in weakness; it is raised in power:

It is sown a natural body; it is raised a spiritual body.
There is a natural body, and there is a spiritual body.

And so it is written,
The first man Adam was made a living soul;
the last Adam *was made* a quickening spirit.

There is one glory

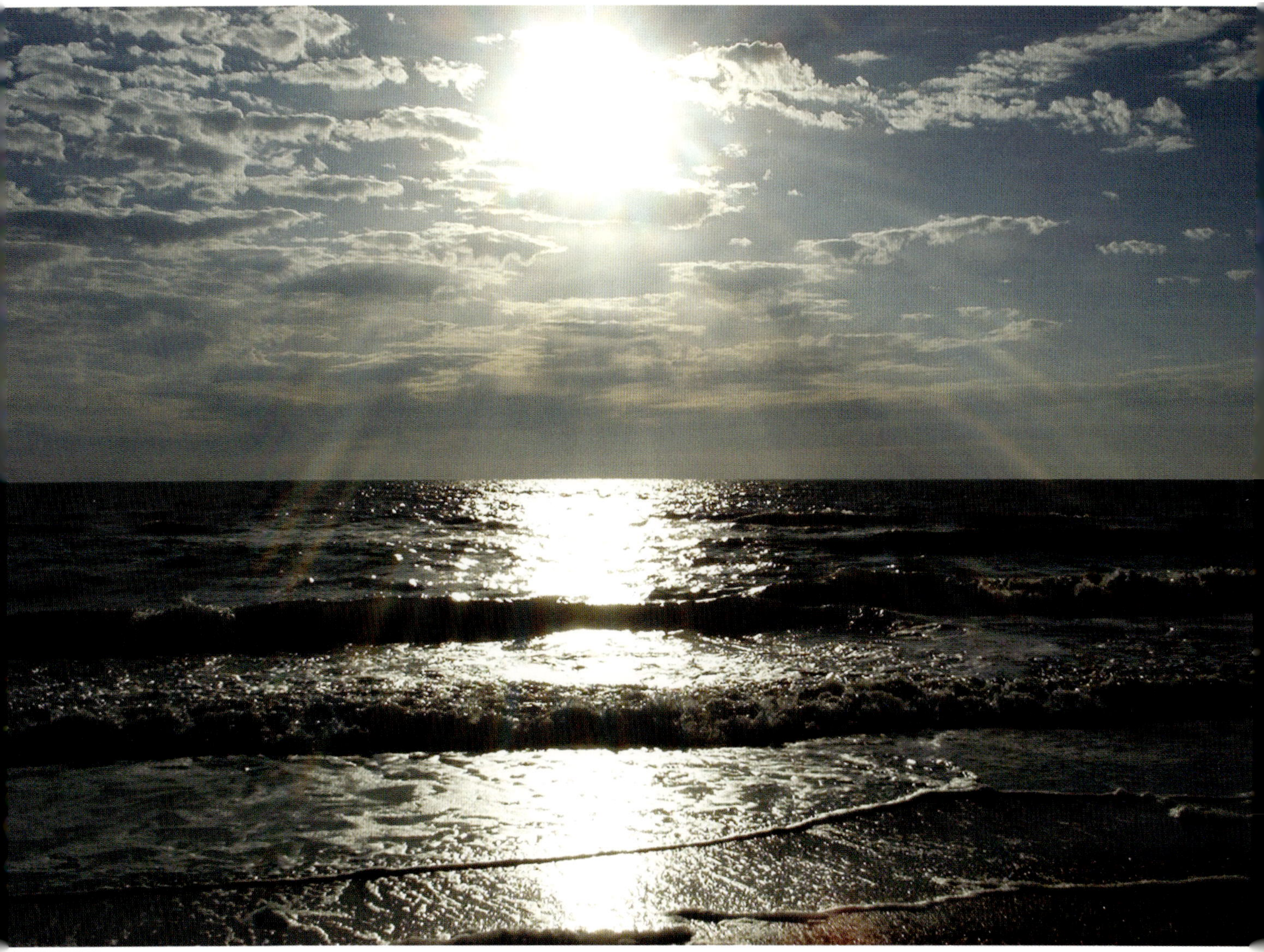

of the sun

2 Corinthians 4 : 3-10

But if our gospel be hid, it is hid to them that are lost:

In whom the god of this world hath blinded the minds of them which believe not,
lest the light of the glorious gospel of Christ,
who is the image of God, should shine unto them.

For we preach not ourselves, but Christ Jesus the Lord;
and ourselves your servants for Jesus' sake.

For God, who commanded the light to shine out of darkness,
hath shined in our hearts,
to *give* the light of the knowledge of the glory of God in the face of Jesus Christ.

But we have this treasure in earthen vessels,
that the excellency of the power may be of God,
and not of us.

We are troubled on every side, yet not distressed;
we are perplexed, but not in despair;

Persecuted, but not forsaken;
cast down, but not destroyed;

Always bearing about in the body the dying of the Lord Jesus,
that the life also of Jesus might be made manifest in our body.

For God, who commanded the light to shine

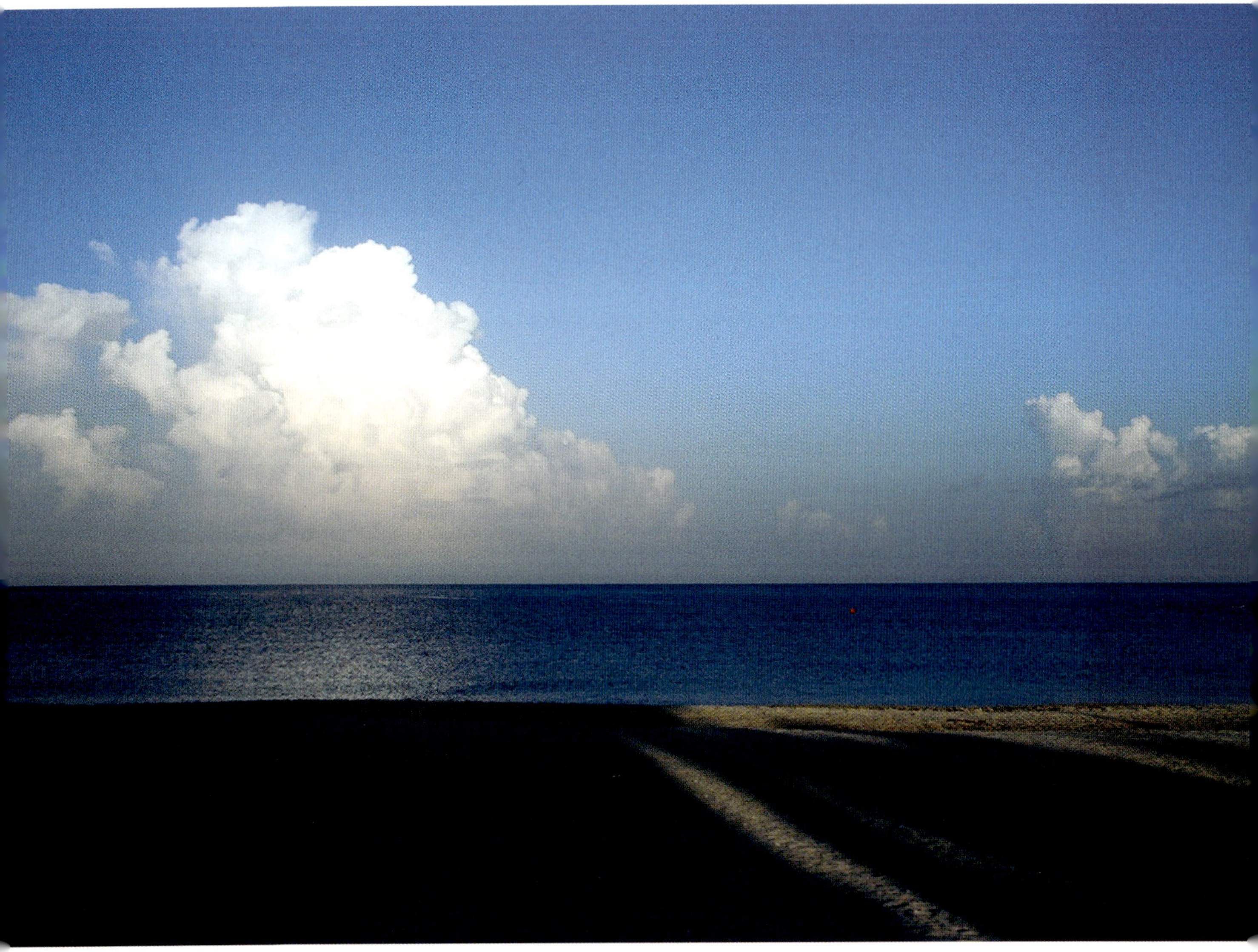

out of darkness

Galatians 3 : 8-14

And the scripture,
forseeing that God would justify the heathen through faith,
preached before the gospel unto Abraham, *saying,*
In thee shall all nations be blessed.

So then they which be of faith are blessed with faithful Abraham.

For as many as are of the works of the law are under the curse: for it is written,
Cursed *is* every one that continueth not in all things which are written
in the book of the law to do them.

But that no man is justified by the law in the sight of God, *it is* evident: for,
The just shall live by faith.

And the law is not of faith: but,
The man that doeth them shall live in them.

Christ hath redeemed us from the curse of the law,
being made a curse for us: for it is written,
Cursed *is* every one that hangeth on a tree:

That the blessing of Abraham might come on the Gentiles through Jesus Christ;
that we might receive the promise of the Spirit through faith.

For it is written,

c
u
r
s
e
d

is every one

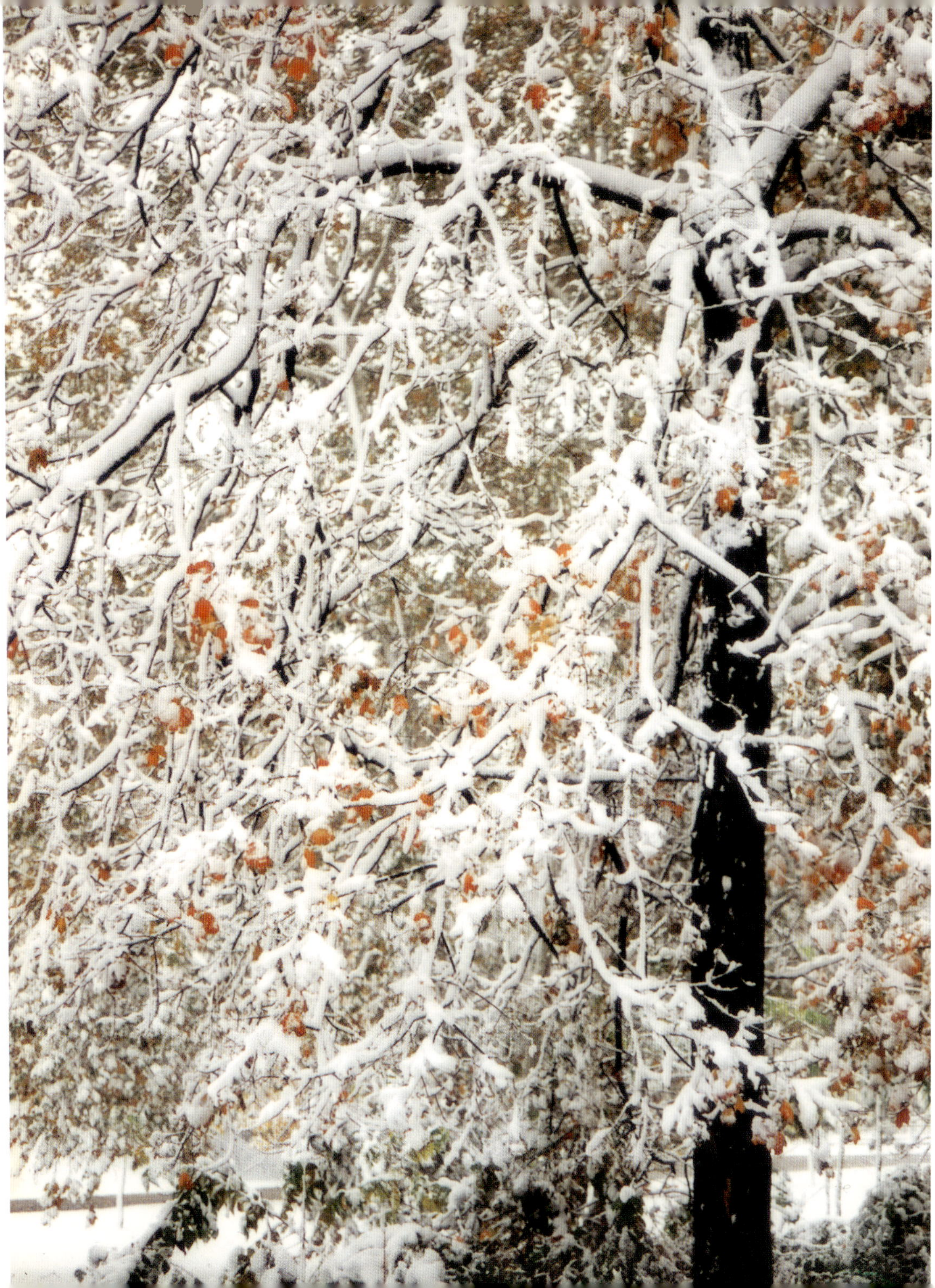

that

h
a
n
g
e
t
h

on a tree

Ephesians 2 : 13-22

But now in Christ Jesus
ye who sometimes were far off are made nigh by the blood of Christ.

For he is our peace, who hath made both one,
and hath broken down the middle wall of partition *between us;*

Having abolished in his flesh the enmity,
even the law of commandments *contained* in ordinances;
for to make in himself of twain one new man, *so* making peace;

And that he might reconcile both unto God in one body by the cross,
having slain the enmity thereby:

And came and preached peace to you which were afar off, and to them that were nigh.

For through him we both have access by one Spirit unto the Father.

Now therefore ye are no more strangers and foreigners,
but fellowcitizens with the saints, and of the household of God;

And are built upon the foundation of the apostles and prophets,
Jesus Christ himself being the chief corner *stone;*

In whom all the building fitly framed together groweth unto an holy temple in the Lord:

In whom ye also are builded together for an habitation of God through the Spirit.

econcile
oth
nto
od

ne
ody

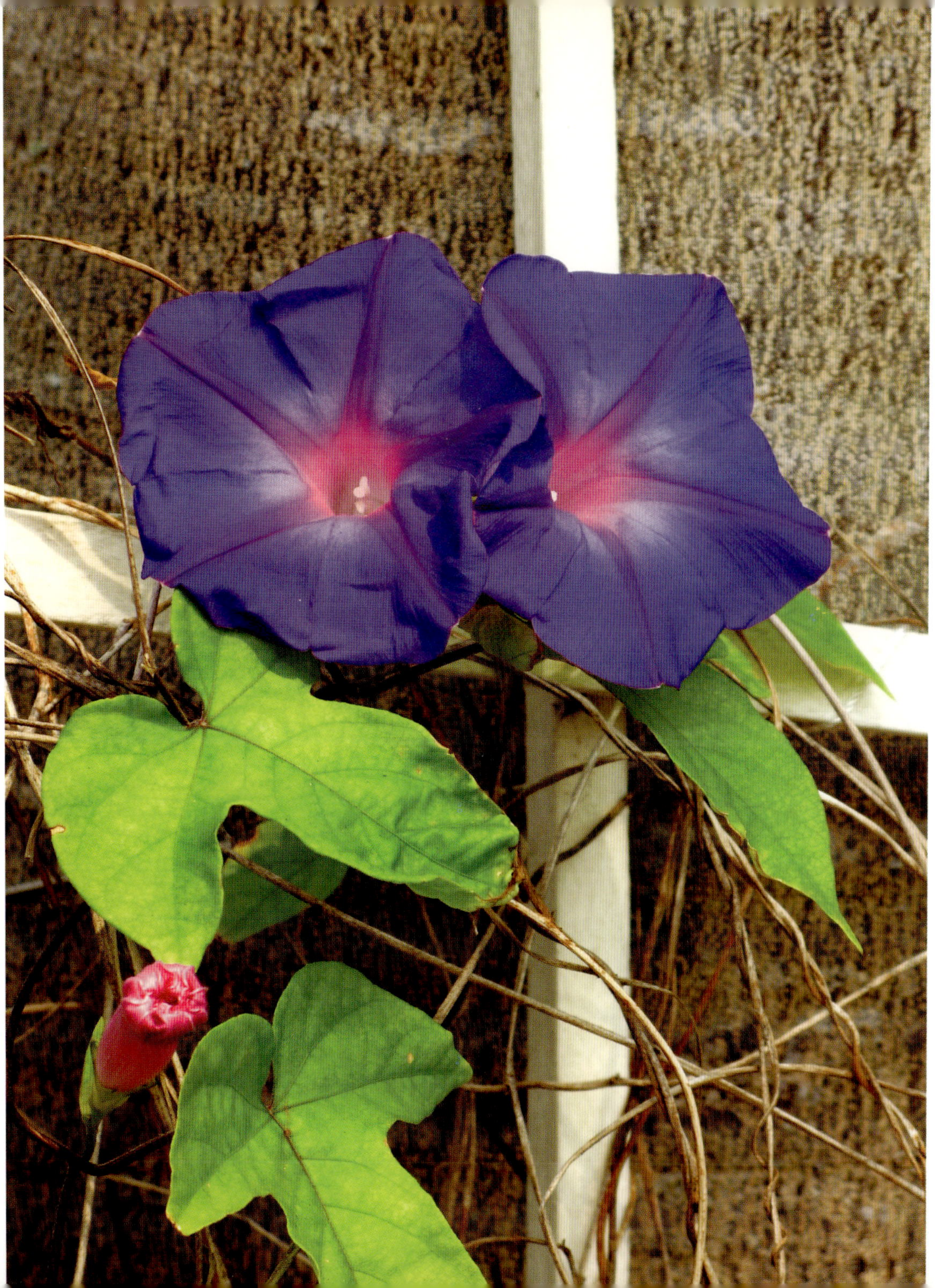

by
the
cross

Philippians 4 : 8-13

Finally, brethren, whatsoever things are true, whatsoever things *are* honest,
whatsoever things *are* just, whatsoever things *are* pure,
whatsoever things *are* lovely, whatsoever things *are* of good report;
if *there be* any virtue, and if *there be* any praise,
think on these things.

Those things,
which ye have both learned, and received, and heard, and seen in me,
do:
and the God of peace shall be with you.

But I rejoiced in the Lord greatly,
that now at the last your care of me hath flourished again;
wherein ye were also careful, but ye lacked opportunity.

Not that I speak in respect of want:
for I have learned, in whatsoever state I am,
therewith to be content.

I know both how to be abased, and I know how to abound:
every where and in all things I am instructed both to be full and to be hungry,
both to abound and to suffer need.

I can do all things through Christ which strengtheneth me.

whatsoever things *are* pure,

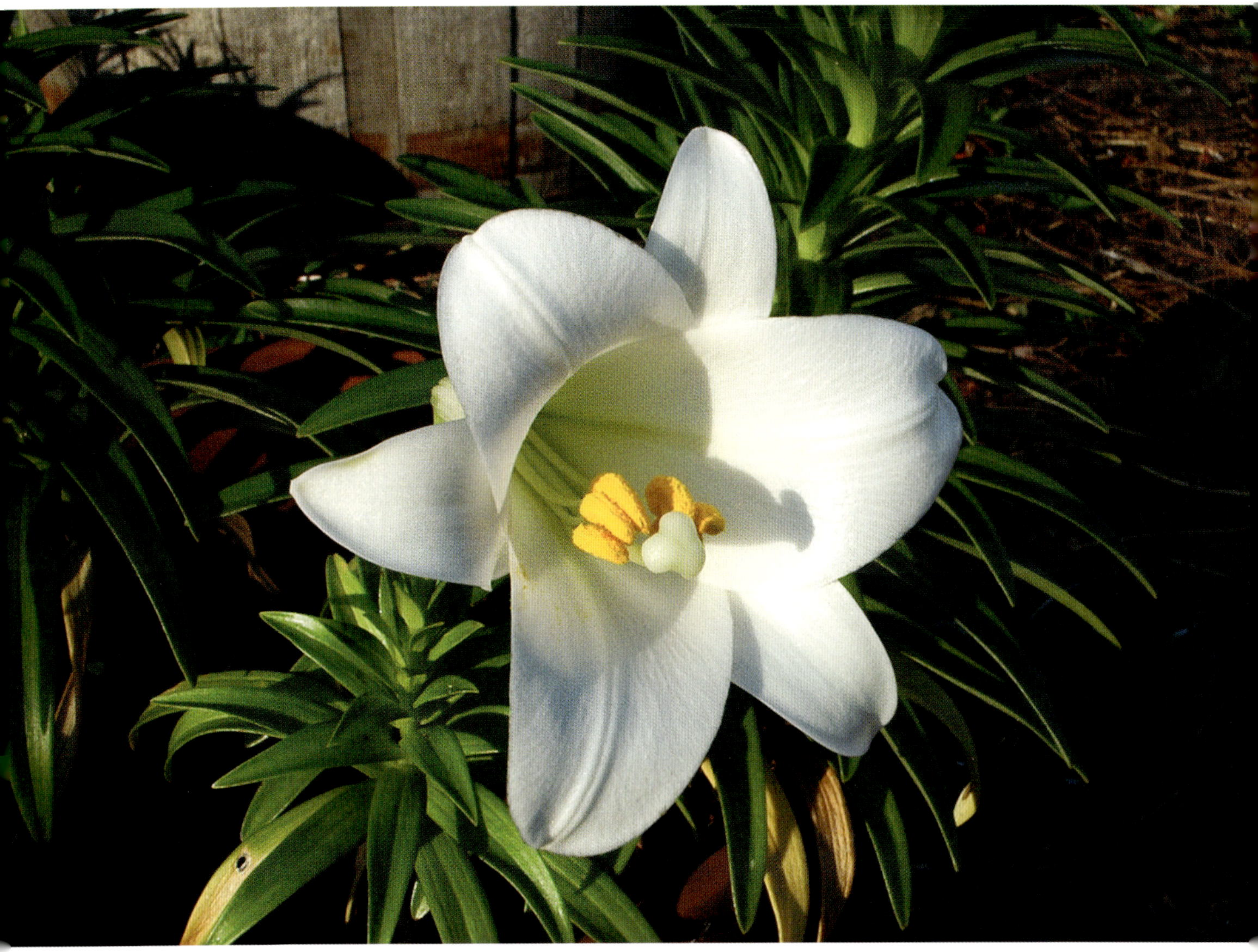

whatsoever things *are* lovely

Colossians 2 : 8-17

Beware lest any man spoil you through philosophy and vain deceit,
after the tradition of men, after the rudiments of the world, and not after Christ.

For in him dwelleth all the fulness of the Godhead bodily.

And ye are complete in him, which is the head of all principality and power:

In whom also ye are circumcised with the circumcision made without hands,
in putting off the body of the sins of the flesh by the circumcision of Christ:

Buried with him in baptism, wherein also ye are risen with *him*
through the faith of the operation of God, who hath raised him from the dead.

And you, being dead in your sins and the uncircumcision of your flesh,
hath he quickened together with him, having forgiven you all trespasses;

Blotting out the handwriting of ordinances that was against us,
which was contrary to us, and took it out of the way, nailing it to his cross;

And having spoiled principalities and powers, he made a shew of them openly,
triumphing over them in it.

Let no man therefore judge you in meat, or in drink, or in respect of an holyday,
or of the new moon, or of the sabbath *days*:

Which are a shadow of things to come; but the body *is* of Christ.

Which
are a

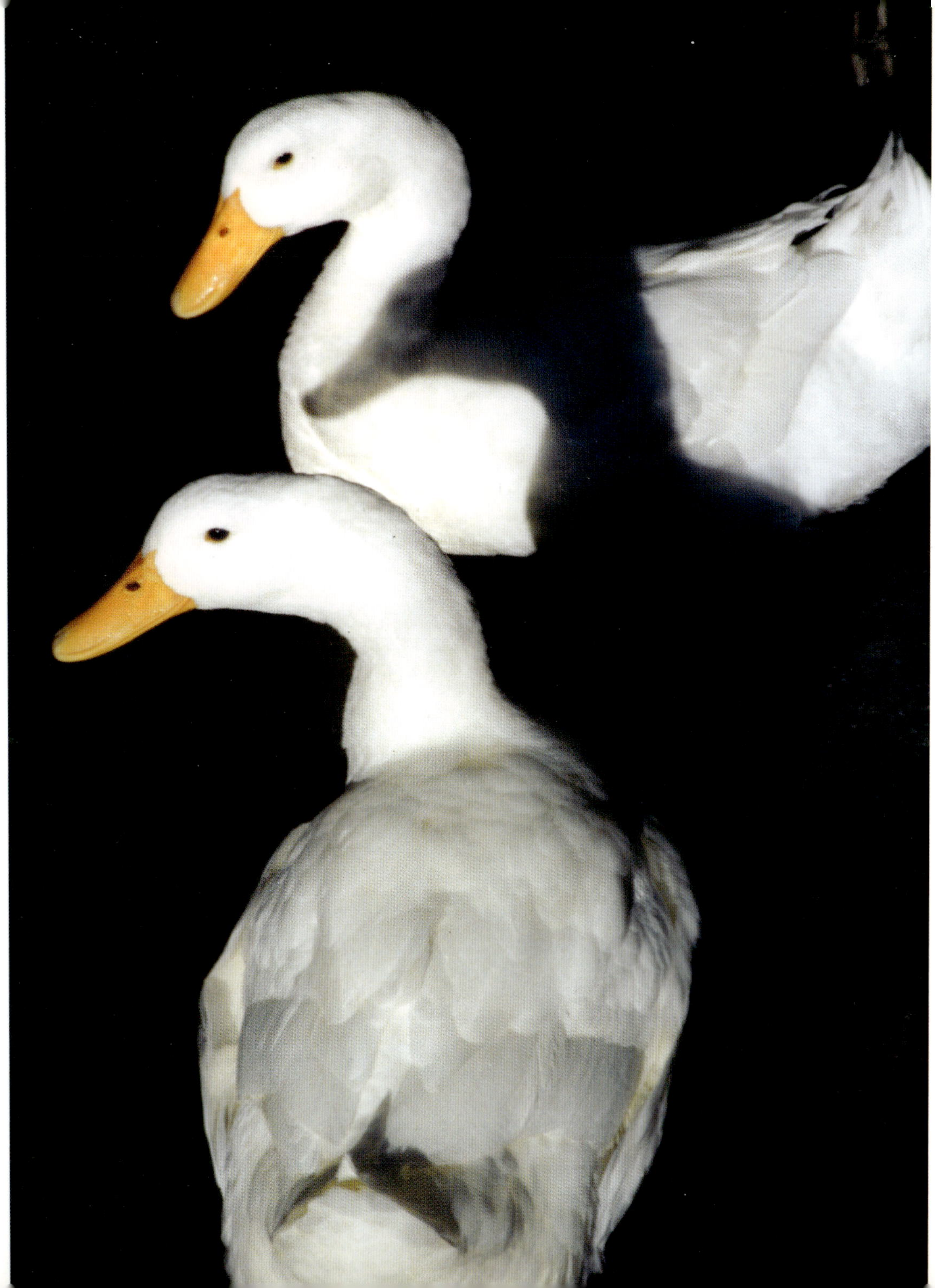

s
h
a
d
o
w

s
h
a
d
o
w

of
things
to come

1 Thessalonians 4 : 13-18

But I would not have you to be ignorant, brethren,
concerning them which are asleep,
that ye sorrow not,
even as others which have no hope.

For if we believe that Jesus died and rose again,
even so them also which sleep in Jesus will God bring with him.

For this we say unto you by the word of the Lord,
that we which are alive *and* remain unto the coming of the Lord
shall not prevent them which are asleep.

For the Lord himself shall descend from heaven with a shout,
with the voice of the archangel,
and with the trump of God:
and the dead in Christ shall rise first:

Then we which are alive *and* remain
shall be caught up together with them in the clouds
to meet the Lord in the air:
and so shall we ever be with the Lord.

Wherefore comfort one another with these words.

ve which are alive *and* remain shall be caught up together with them in the clouds

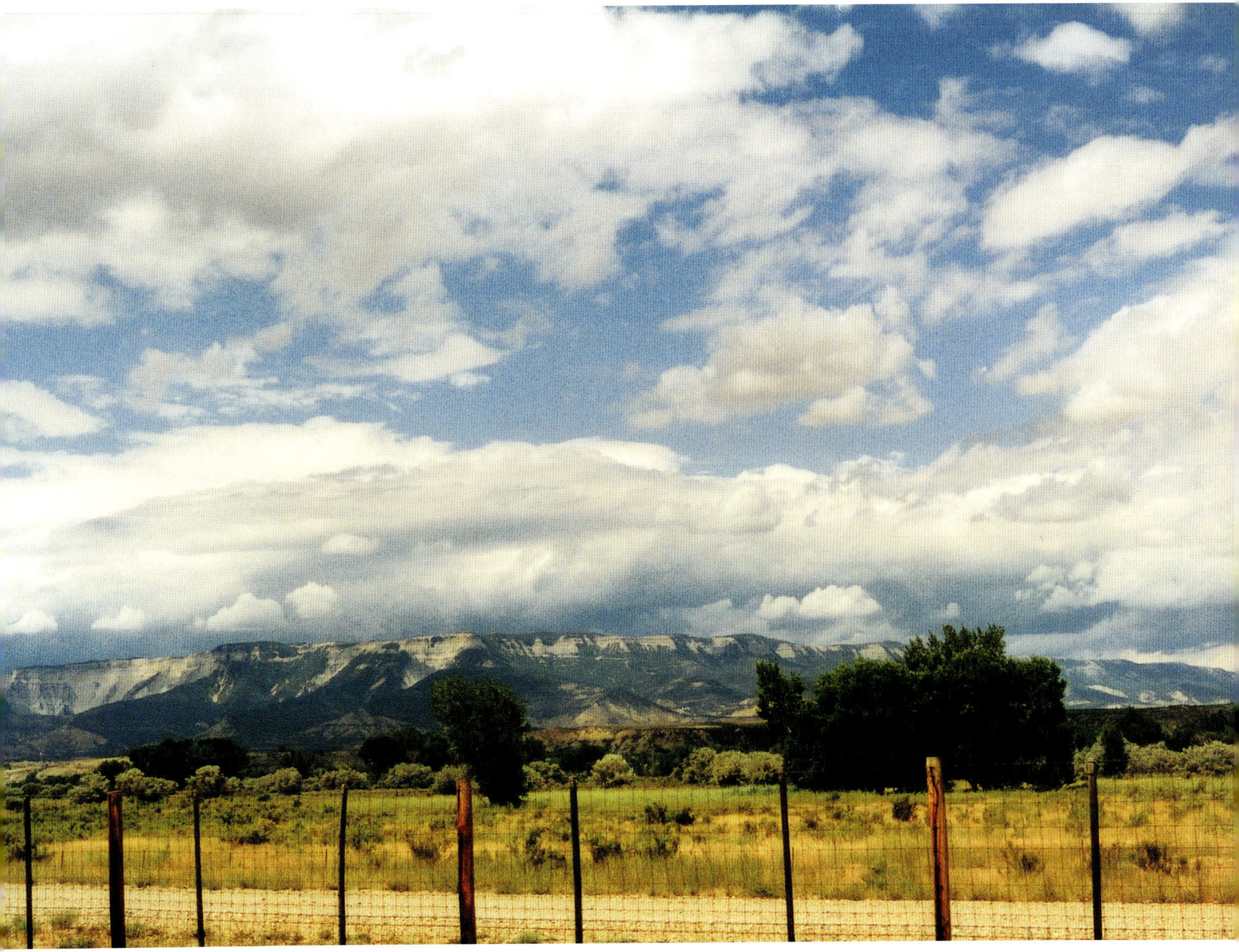

to meet the Lord in the air

2 Thessalonians 3 : 1-5

Finally, brethren,
pray for us,
that the word of the Lord may have *free* course,
and be glorified,
even as *it is* with you:

And that we may be delivered from unreasonable and wicked men:
for all *men* have not faith.

But the Lord is faithful,
who shall stablish you,
and keep *you* from evil.

And we have confidence in the Lord touching you,
that ye both do and will do the things which we command you.

And the Lord direct your hearts into the love of God,
and into the patient waiting for Christ.

and into the patient w a i t i n g

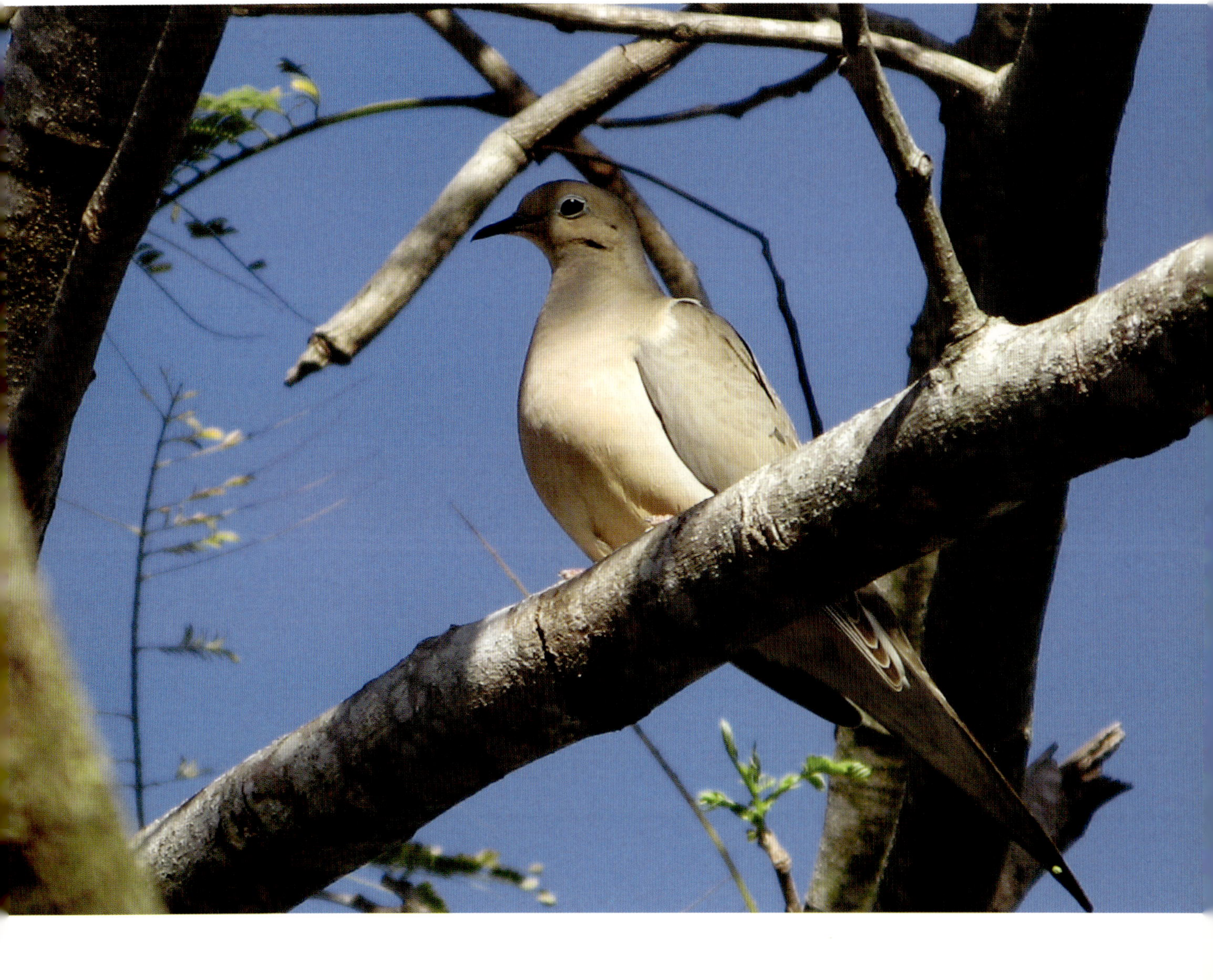

for Christ

1 Timothy 4 : 1-6

Now the Spirit speaketh expressly,
that in the latter times some shall depart from the faith,
giving heed to seducing spirits, and doctrines of devils;

Speaking lies in hypocrisy;
having their conscience seared with a hot iron;

Forbidding to marry,
and commanding to abstain from meats,
which God hath created to be received with thanksgiving
of them which believe and know the truth.

For every creature of God *is* good,
and nothing to be refused,
if it be received with thanksgiving:

For it is sanctified by the word of God and prayer.

If thou put the brethren in remembrance of these things,
thou shalt be a good minister of Jesus Christ,
nourished up in the words of faith and of good doctrine,
whereunto thou hast attained.

For every creature of God

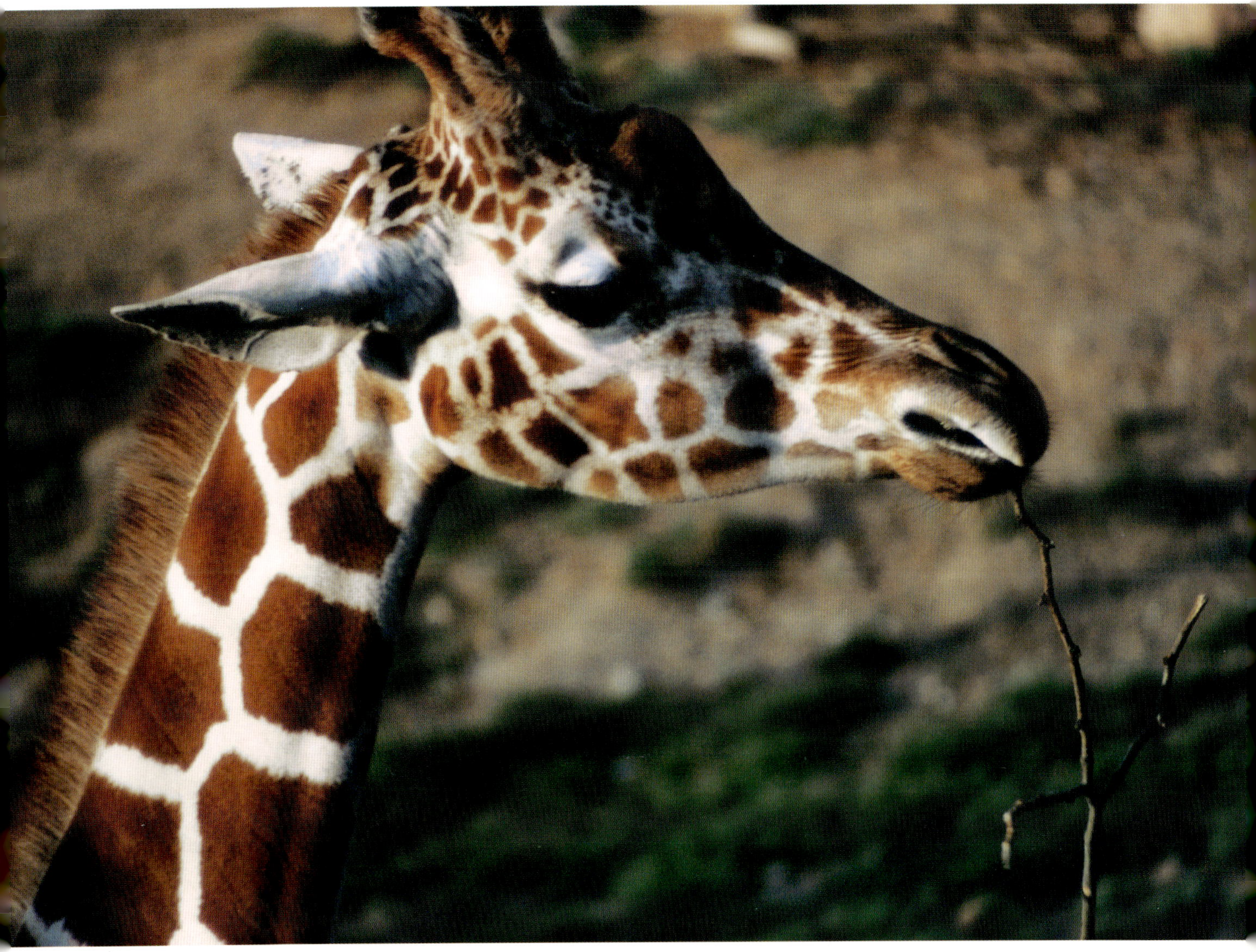

is good

2 Timothy 2 : 1-10

Thou therefore, my son, be strong in the grace that is in Christ Jesus.

And the things that thou hast heard of me among many witnesses,
the same commit thou to faithful men, who shall be able to teach others also.

Thou therefore endure hardness, as a good soldier of Jesus Christ.

No man that warreth entangle himself with the affairs of *this* life;
that he may please him who hath chosen him to be a soldier.

And if a man also strive for masteries, *yet* is he not crowned, except he strive lawfully.

The husbandman that laboureth must be first partaker of the fruits.

Consider what I say; and the Lord give thee understanding in all things.

Remember that Jesus Christ of the seed of David was raised from the dead
according to my gospel:

Wherein I suffer trouble, as an evil doer, *even* unto bonds;
but the word of God is not bound.

Therefore I endure all things for the elect's sakes,
that they may also obtain the salvation which is in Christ Jesus with eternal glory.

No man that warreth entangleth himself

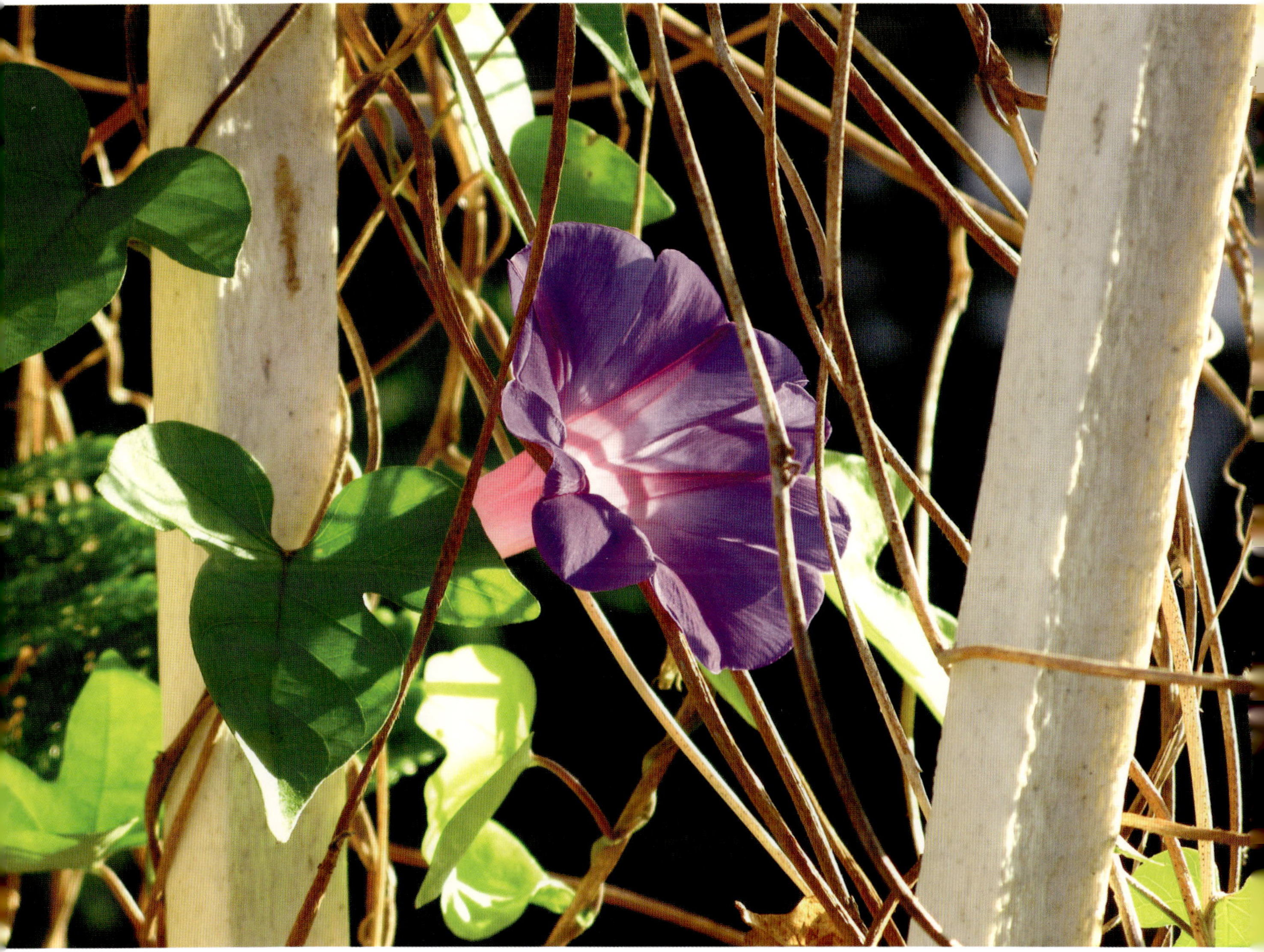

with the affairs of *this* life

Titus 3 : 5-11

Not by works of righteousness which we have done,
but according to his mercy he saved us,
by the washing of regeneration,
and renewing of the Holy Ghost;

Which he shed on us abundantly through Jesus Christ our Saviour;

That being justified by his grace,
we should be made heirs according to the hope of eternal life.

This is a faithful saying, and these things I will that thou affirm constantly,
that they which have believed in God might be careful to maintain good works.
These things are good and profitable unto men.

But avoid foolish questions,
and genealogies, and contentions,
and strivings about the law;
for they are unprofitable and vain.

A man that is an heretick after the first and second admonition reject;

Knowing that he that is such is subverted, and sinneth,
being condemned of himself.

by the washing

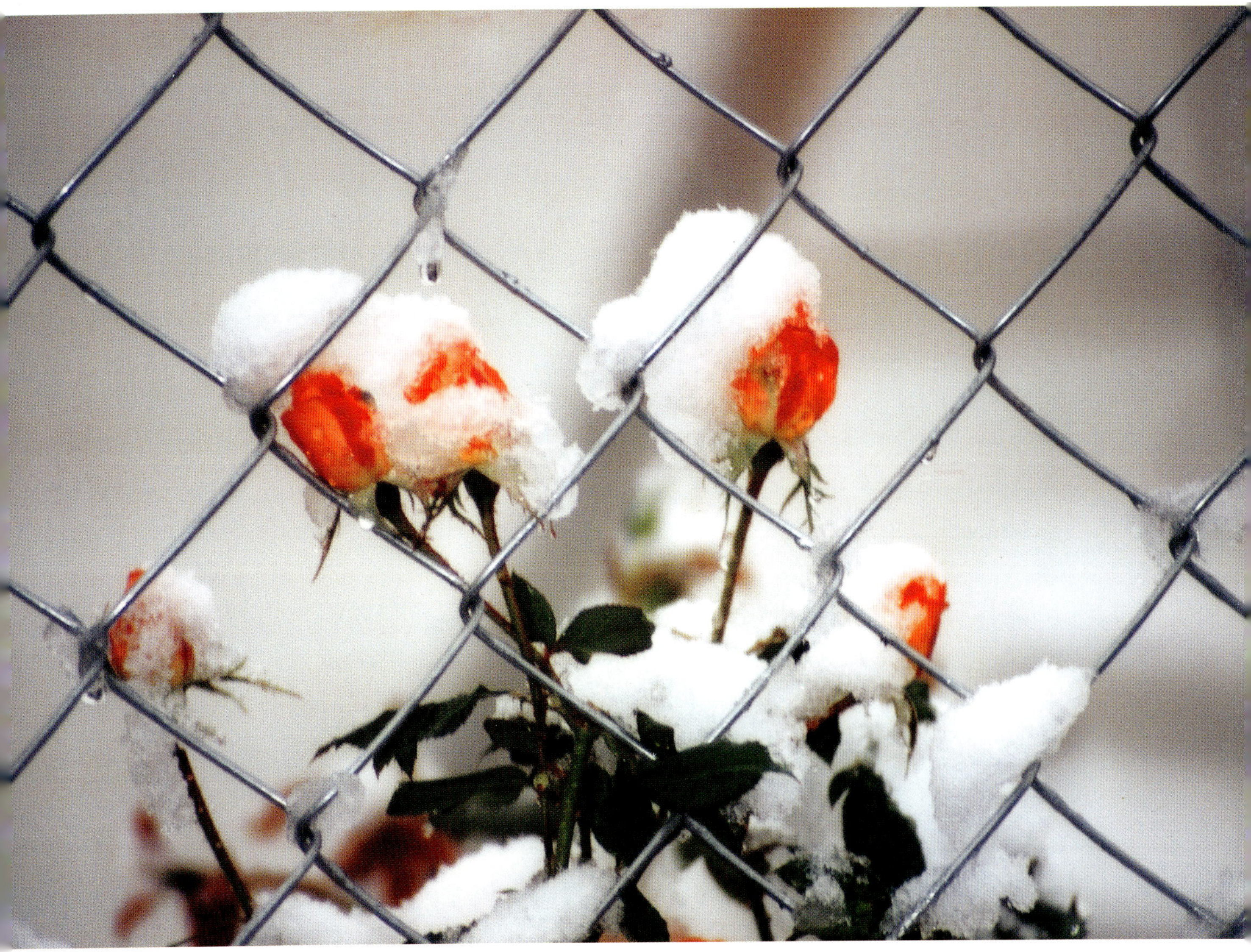

of regeneration

Philemon 1 : 1-7

Paul,
a prisoner of Jesus Christ,
and Timothy *our* brother,
unto Philemon our dearly beloved,
and fellowlabourer,

And to *our* beloved Apphia, and Archippus our fellowsoldier,
and to the church in thy house:

Grace to you, and peace,
from God our Father and the Lord Jesus Christ.

I thank my God,
making mention of thee always in my prayers,

Hearing of thy love and faith,
which thou hast toward the Lord Jesus,
and toward all saints;

That the communication of thy faith may become effectual
by the acknowledging of every good thing
which is in you in Christ Jesus.

For we have great joy and consolation in thy love,
because the bowels of the saints are refreshed by thee, brother.

Grace to you, and peace,

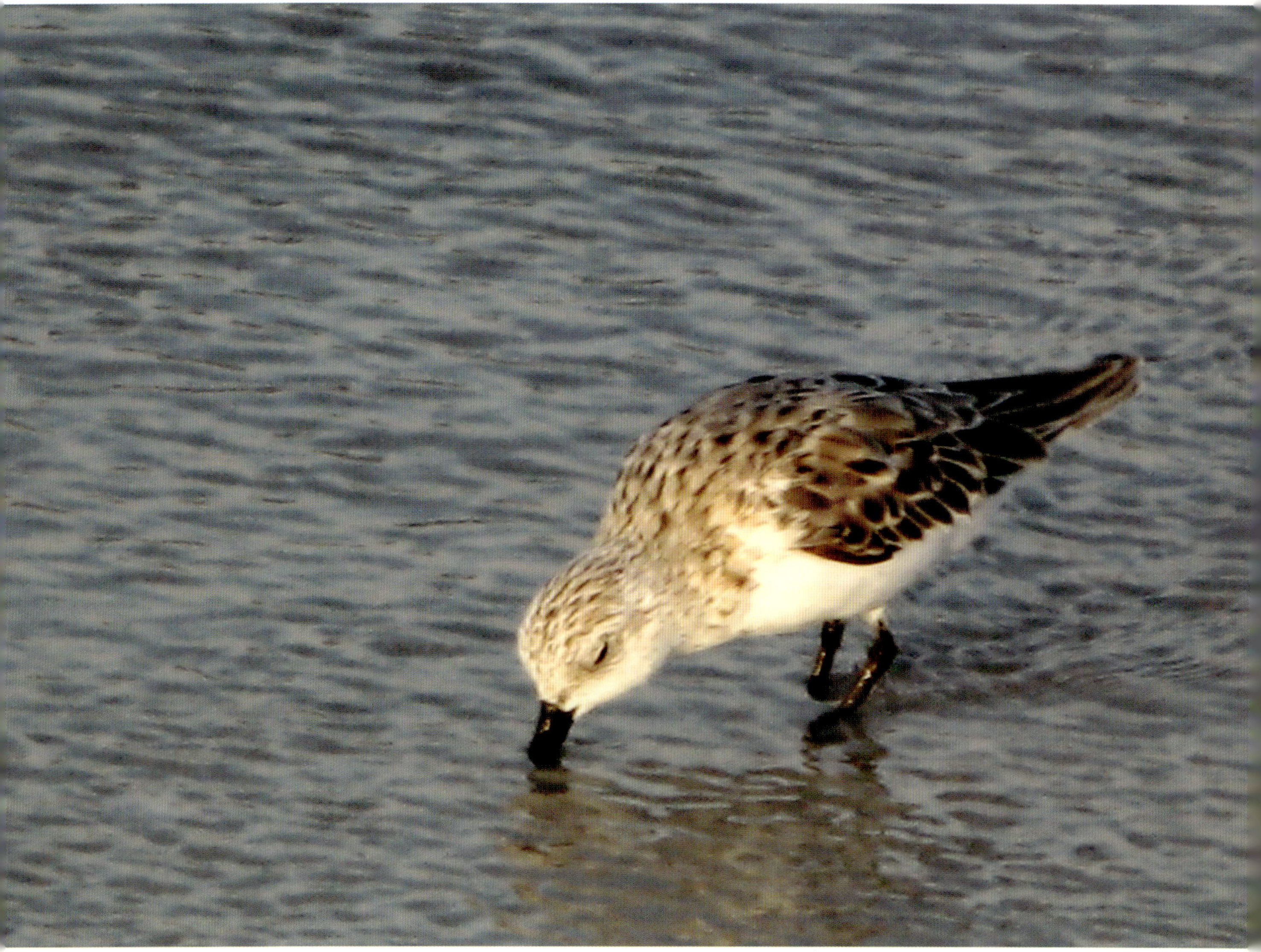

from God our Father and the Lord Jesus Christ

Hebrews 12 : 1-3

Wherefore seeing we also are compassed about
with so great a cloud of witnesses,
let us lay aside every weight,
and the sin which doth so easily beset *us,*
and let us run with patience the race that is set before us.

Looking unto Jesus the author and finisher of *our* faith;
who for the joy that was set before him endured the cross,
despising the shame,
and is set down at the right hand of the throne of God.

For consider him that endured such contradiction of sinners against himself,
lest ye be wearied and faint in your minds.

Wherefore seeing we also are compassed about

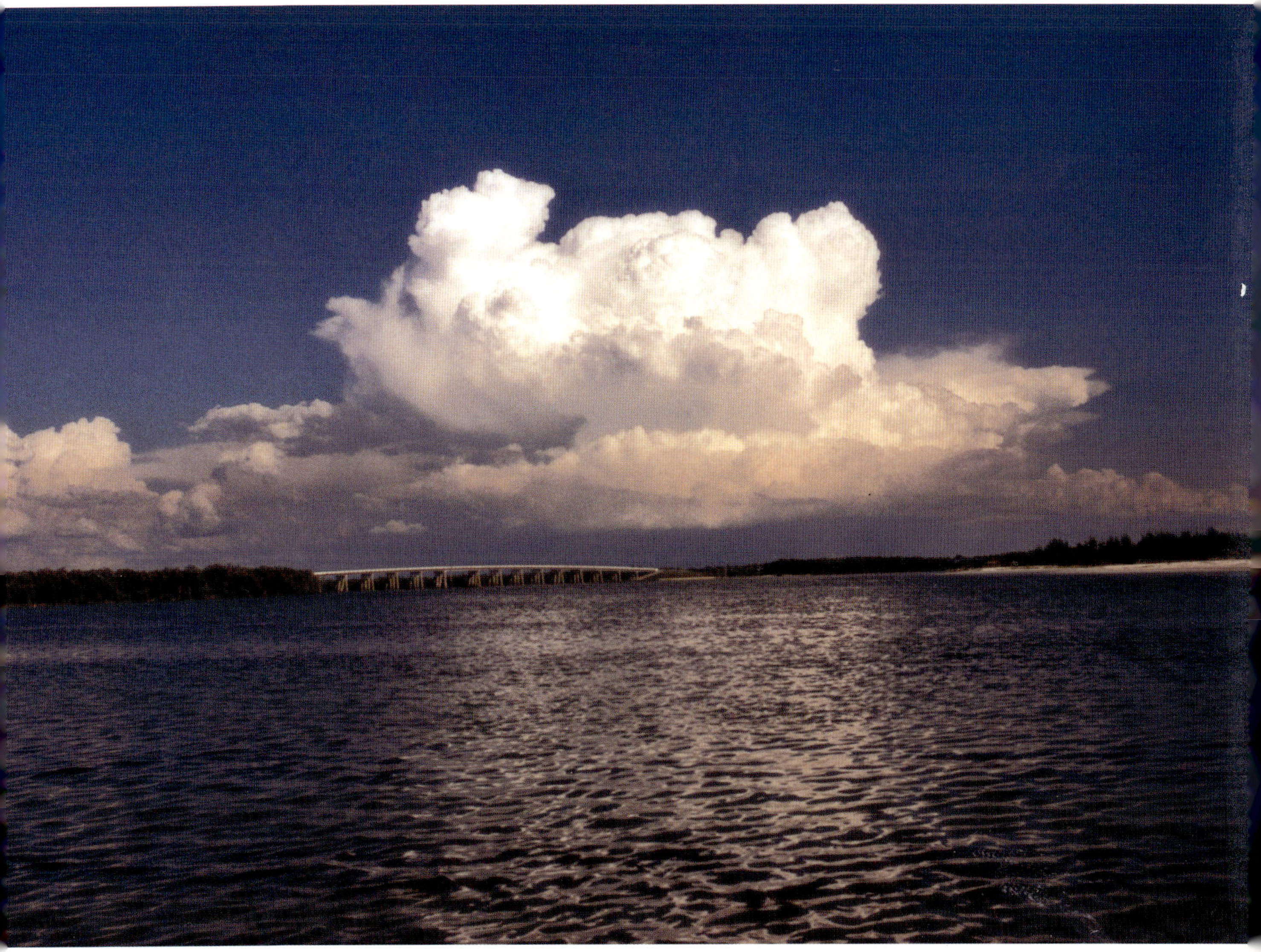

with so great a cloud of witnesses

James 1 : 2-8

My brethren,
count it all joy when ye fall into divers temptations;

Knowing *this*, that the trying of your faith worketh patience.

But let patience have *her* perfect work,
that ye may be perfect and entire,
wanting nothing.

If any of you lack wisdom, let him ask of God,
that giveth to all *men* liberally, and upbraideth not;
and it shall be given him.

But let him ask in faith, nothing wavering.
For he that wavereth is like a wave of the sea
driven with the wind and tossed.

For let not that man think that he shall receive any thing of the Lord.

A double minded man *is* unstable in all his ways.

For he that wavereth is like a wave of the sea

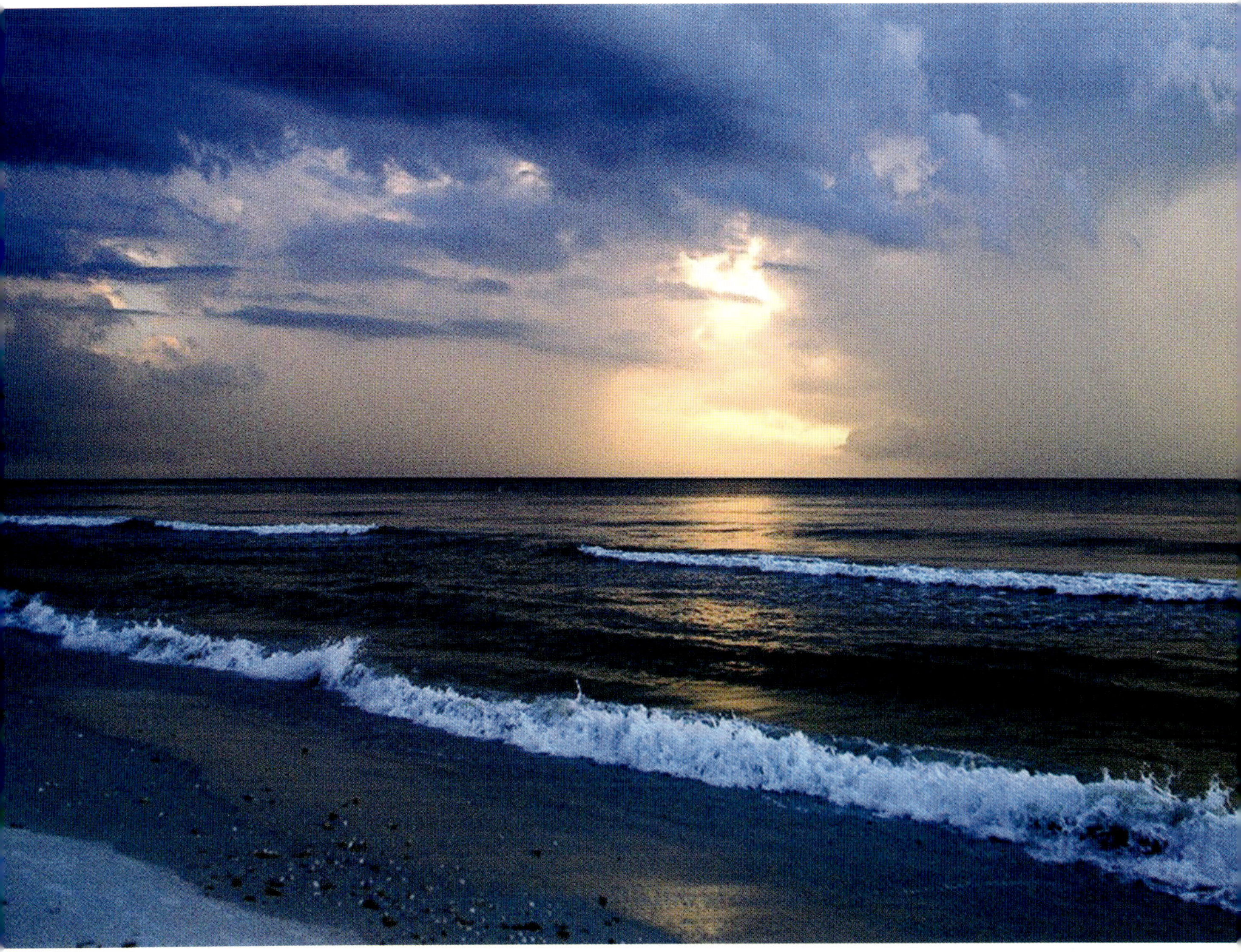

driven with the wind and tossed

1 Peter 2 : 1-8

Wherefore laying aside all malice, and all guile, and hypocrisies,
and envies, and all evil speakings,

As newborn babes, desire the sincere milk of the word,
that ye may grow thereby:

If so be ye have tasted that the Lord *is* gracious.

To whom coming, *as unto* a living stone,
disallowed indeed of men, but chosen of God, *and* precious,

Ye also, as lively stones, are built up a spiritual house, an holy priesthood,
to offer up spiritual sacrifices, acceptable to God by Jesus Christ.

Wherefore also it is contained in the scripture,
Behold, I lay in Sion a chief corner stone, elect, precious:
and he that believeth on him shall not be confounded.

Unto you therefore which believe *he is* precious:
but unto them which be disobedient, the stone which the builders disallowed,
the same is made the head of the corner,

And a stone of stumbling, and a rock of offence,
even to them which stumble at the word, being disobedient:
whereunto also they were appointed.

a
stone
of
s
t
u
m
b
l
i
n
g

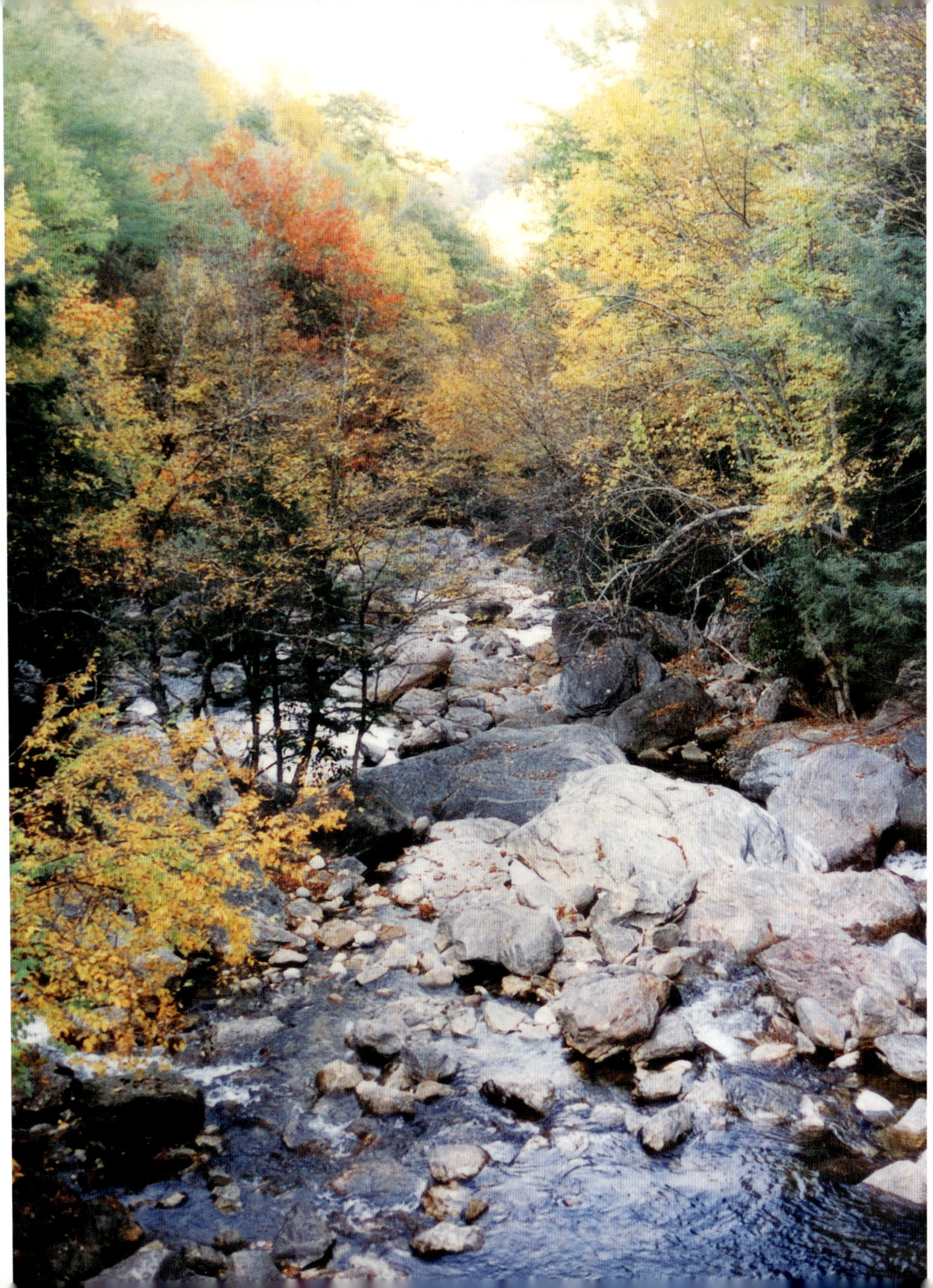

and
a
rock
of
offence

2 Peter 3 : 10-14

But the day of the Lord will come as a thief in the night;
in the which the heavens shall pass away with a great noise,
and the elements shall melt with fervent heat,
the earth also and the works that are therein shall be burned up.

Seeing then *that* all these things shall be dissolved,
what manner *of persons* ought ye to be in *all* holy conversation and godliness,

Looking for and hasting unto the coming of the day of God,
wherein the heavens being on fire shall be dissolved,
and the elements shall melt with fervent heat?

Nevertheless we,
according to his promise,
look for new heavens and a new earth,
wherein dwelleth righteousness.

Wherefore, beloved,
seeing that ye look for such things,
be diligent that ye may be found of him in peace,
without spot, and blameless.

look for new heavens

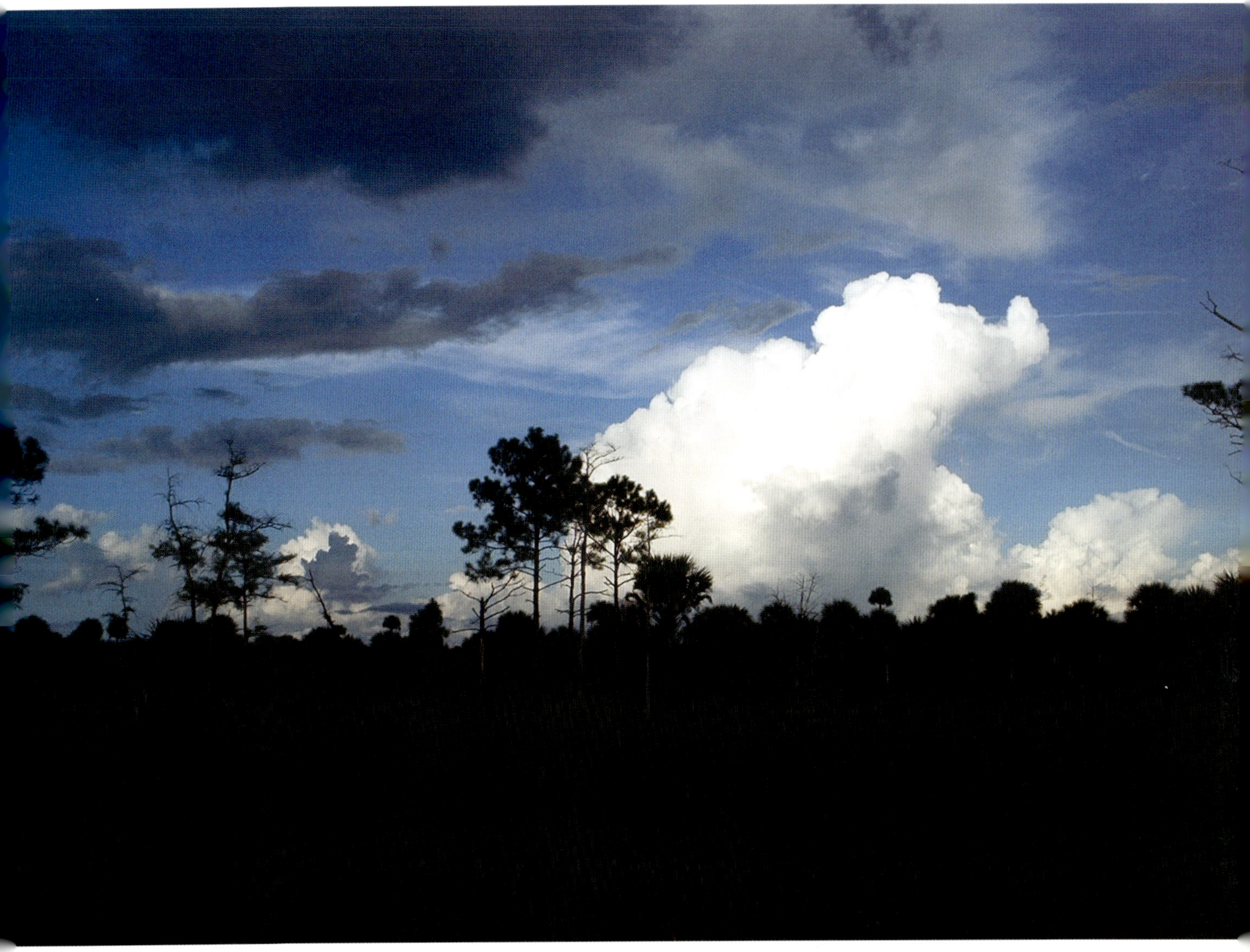

and a new earth

1 John 5 : 4-12

For whatsoever is born of God overcometh the world:
and this is the victory that overcometh the world, *even* our faith.

Who is he that overcometh the world,
but he that believeth that Jesus is the Son of God?

This is he that came by water and blood, *even* Jesus Christ;
not by water only, but by water and blood.
And it is the Spirit that beareth witness, because the Spirit is truth.

For there are three that bear record in heaven,
the Father, the Word, and the Holy Ghost: and these three are one.

And there are three that bear witness in earth,
the spirit, and the water, and the blood: and these three agree in one.

If we receive the witness of men, the witness of God is greater:
for this is the witness of God which he hath testified of his Son.

He that believeth on the Son of God hath the witness in himself:
he that believeth not God hath made him a liar;
because he believeth not the record that God gave of his Son.

And this is the record, that God hath given to us eternal life, and this life is in his Son.

He that hath the Son hath life: *and* he that hath not the Son of God hath not life.

And there are three that bear witness in earth,

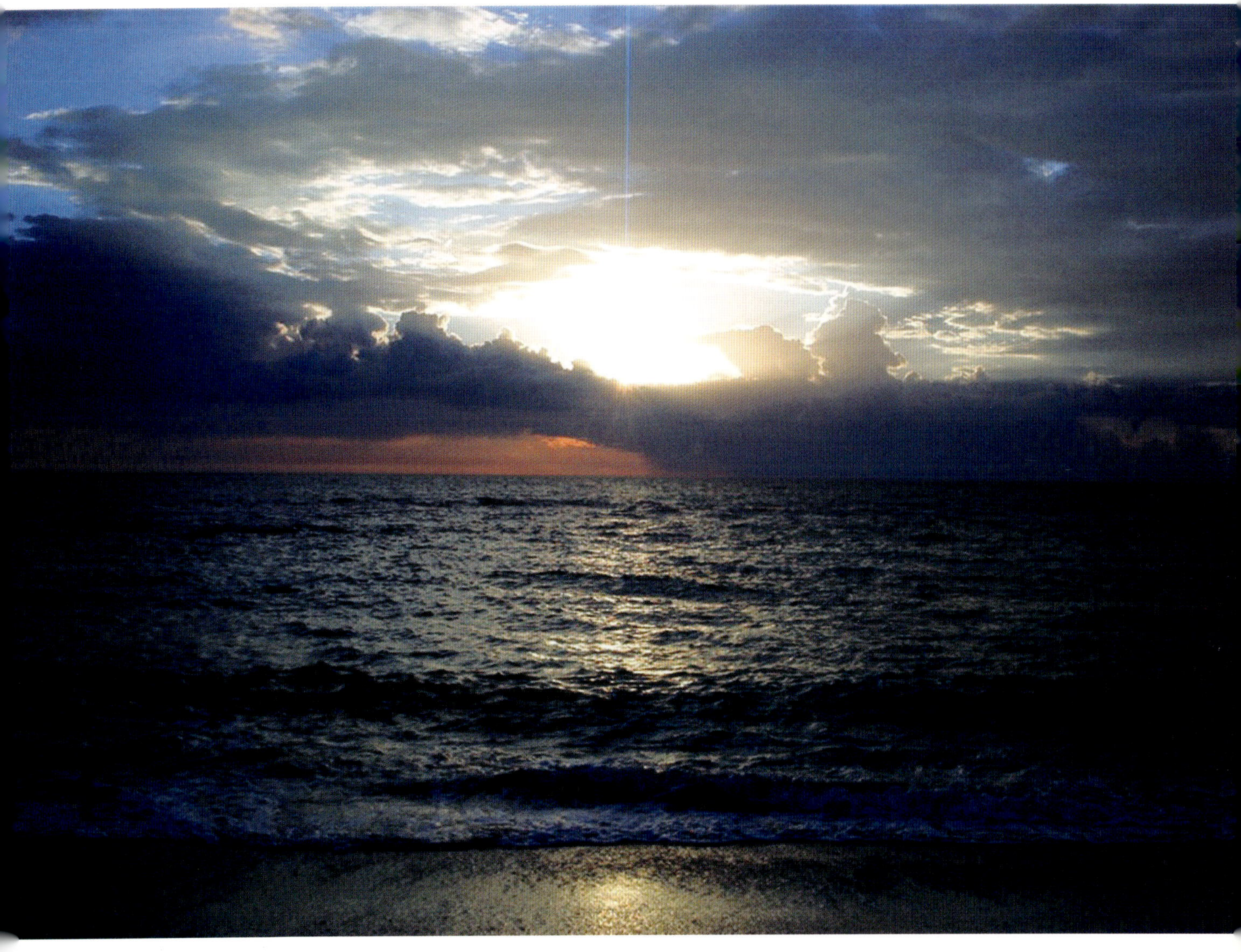

the spirit, and the water, and the blood

2 John 1 : 7-11

For many deceivers are entered into the world,
who confess not that Jesus Christ is come in the flesh.
This is a deceiver and an antichrist.

Look to yourselves,
that we lose not those things which we have wrought,
but that we receive a full reward.

Whosoever transgresseth,
and abideth not in the doctrine of Christ,
hath not God.
He that abideth in the doctrine of Christ,
he hath both the Father and the Son.

If there come any unto you,
and bring not this doctrine,
receive him not into *your* house,
neither bid him God speed:

For he that biddeth him God speed is partaker of his evil deeds.

receive him not

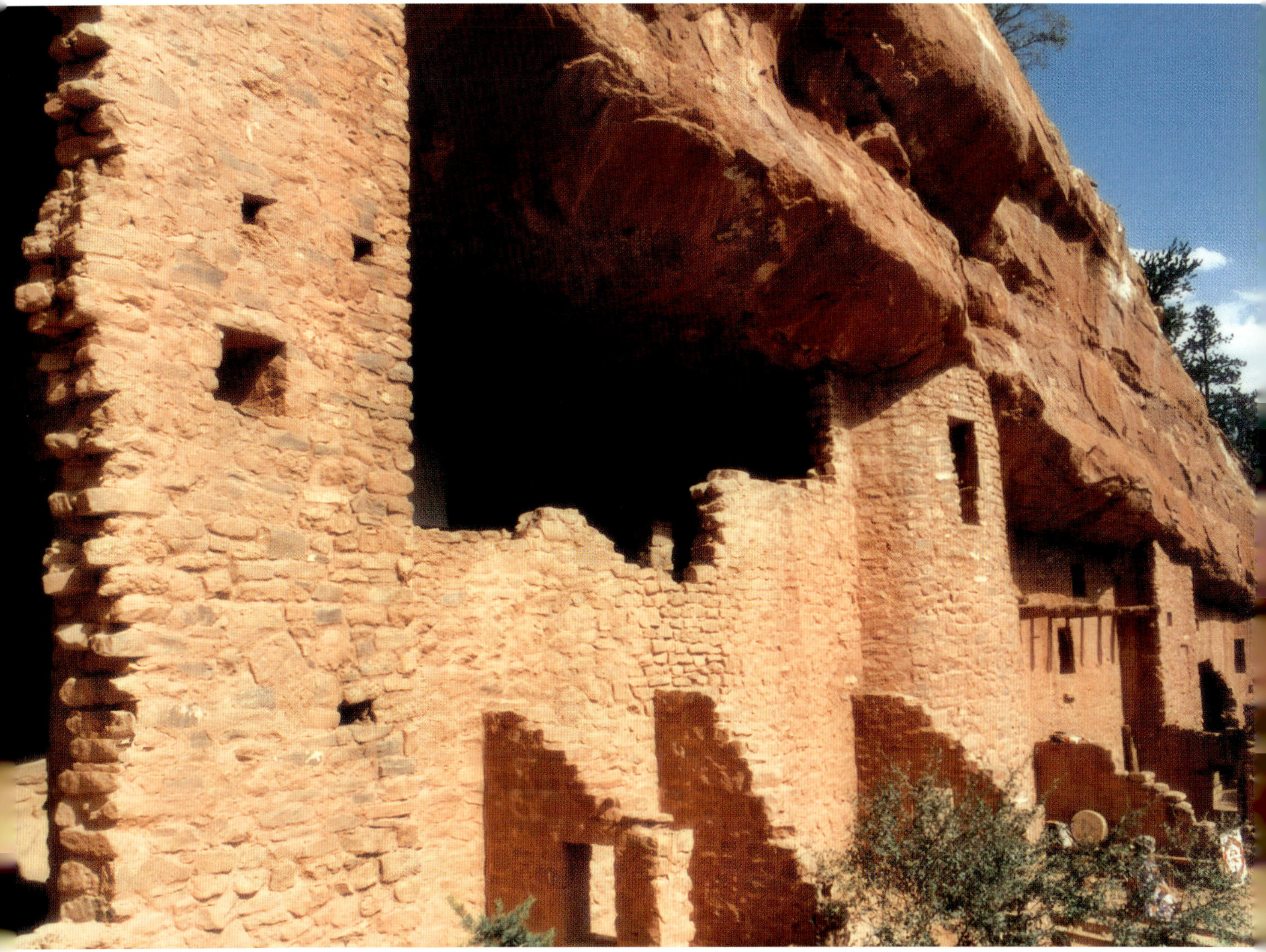

into *your* house

3 John 1 : 2-8

Beloved,
I wish above all things that thou mayest prosper and be in health,
even as thy soul prospereth.

For I rejoiced greatly,
when the brethren came and testified of the truth that is in thee,
even as thou walkest in the truth.

I have no greater joy than to hear that my children walk in truth.

Beloved,
thou doest faithfully whatsoever thou doest to the brethren
and to strangers;

Which have borne witness of thy charity before the church:
whom if thou bring forward on their journey after a godly sort,
thou shalt do well:

Because that for his name's sake they went forth,
taking nothing of the Gentiles.

We therefore ought to receive such,
that we might be fellowhelpers to the truth.

Which have borne witness of thy charity

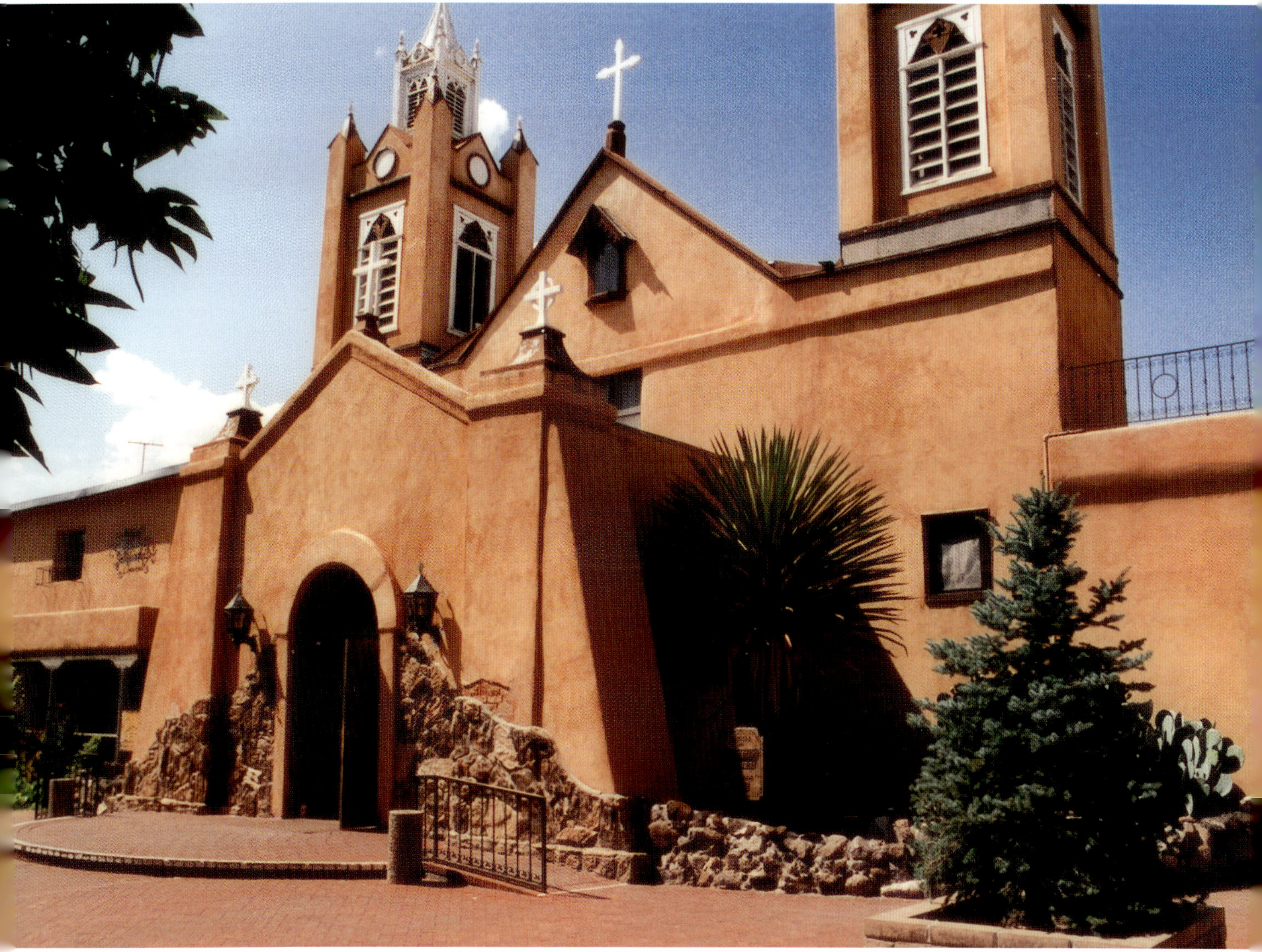

before the church

Jude 1 : 4

For there are certain men crept in unawares,
who were before of old ordained to this condemnation,
ungodly men, turning the grace of our God into lasciviousness,
and denying the only Lord God, and our Lord Jesus Christ.

Jude 1 : 12 -15

These are spots in your feasts of charity,
when they feast with you,
feeding themselves without fear:
clouds *they are* without water, carried about of winds;
trees whose fruit withereth, without fruit,
twice dead, plucked up by the roots;

Raging waves of the sea, foaming out their own shame;
wandering stars, to whom is reserved the blackness of darkness for ever.

And Enoch also, the seventh from Adam,
prophesied of these, saying,
Behold, the Lord cometh with ten thousands of his saints,

To execute judgement upon all,
and to convince all that are ungodly among them of all their ungodly deeds
which they have ungodly committed,
and of all their hard *speeches* which ungodly sinners have spoken against him.

Raging waves of the sea,

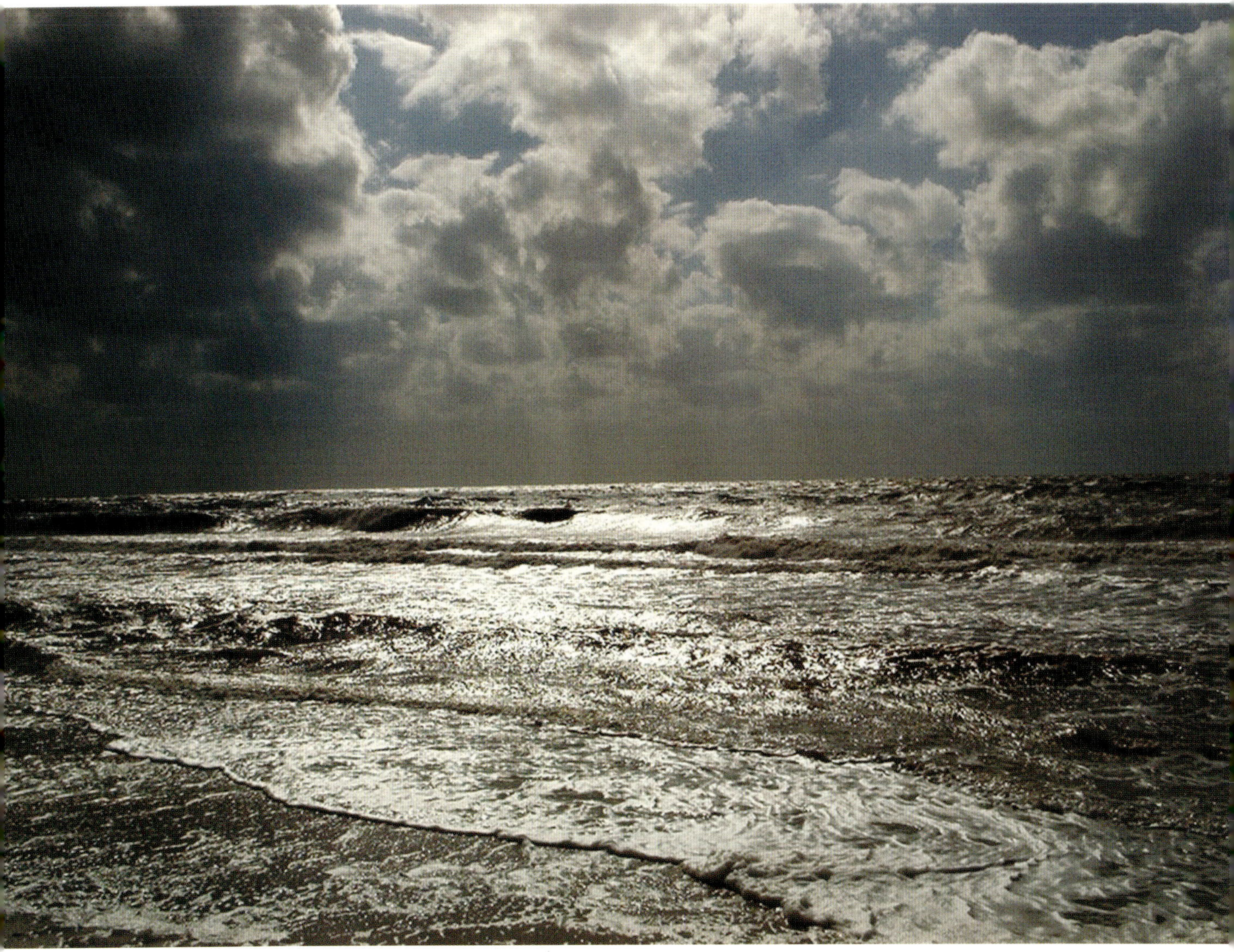

foaming out their own shame

Revelation 21 : 3-7

And I heard a great voice out of heaven saying,
Behold, the tabernacle of God *is* with men,
and he will dwell with them, and they shall be his people,
and God himself shall be with them, *and be* their God.

And God shall wipe away all tears from their eyes;
and there shall be no more death,
neither sorrow, nor crying,
neither shall there be any more pain:
for the former things are passed away.

And he that sat upon the throne said,
BEHOLD, I MAKE ALL THINGS NEW.
And he said unto me,
WRITE: FOR THESE WORDS ARE TRUE AND FAITHFUL.

And he said unto me,
IT IS DONE.
I AM ALPHA AND OMEGA,
THE BEGINNING AND THE END.
I WILL GIVE UNTO HIM THAT IS ATHIRST
OF THE FOUNTAIN OF THE WATER OF LIFE FREELY.

HE THAT OVERCOMETH SHALL INHERIT ALL THINGS;
AND I WILL BE HIS GOD, AND HE SHALL BE MY SON.

I WILL GIVE TO HIM THAT IS ATHIRST

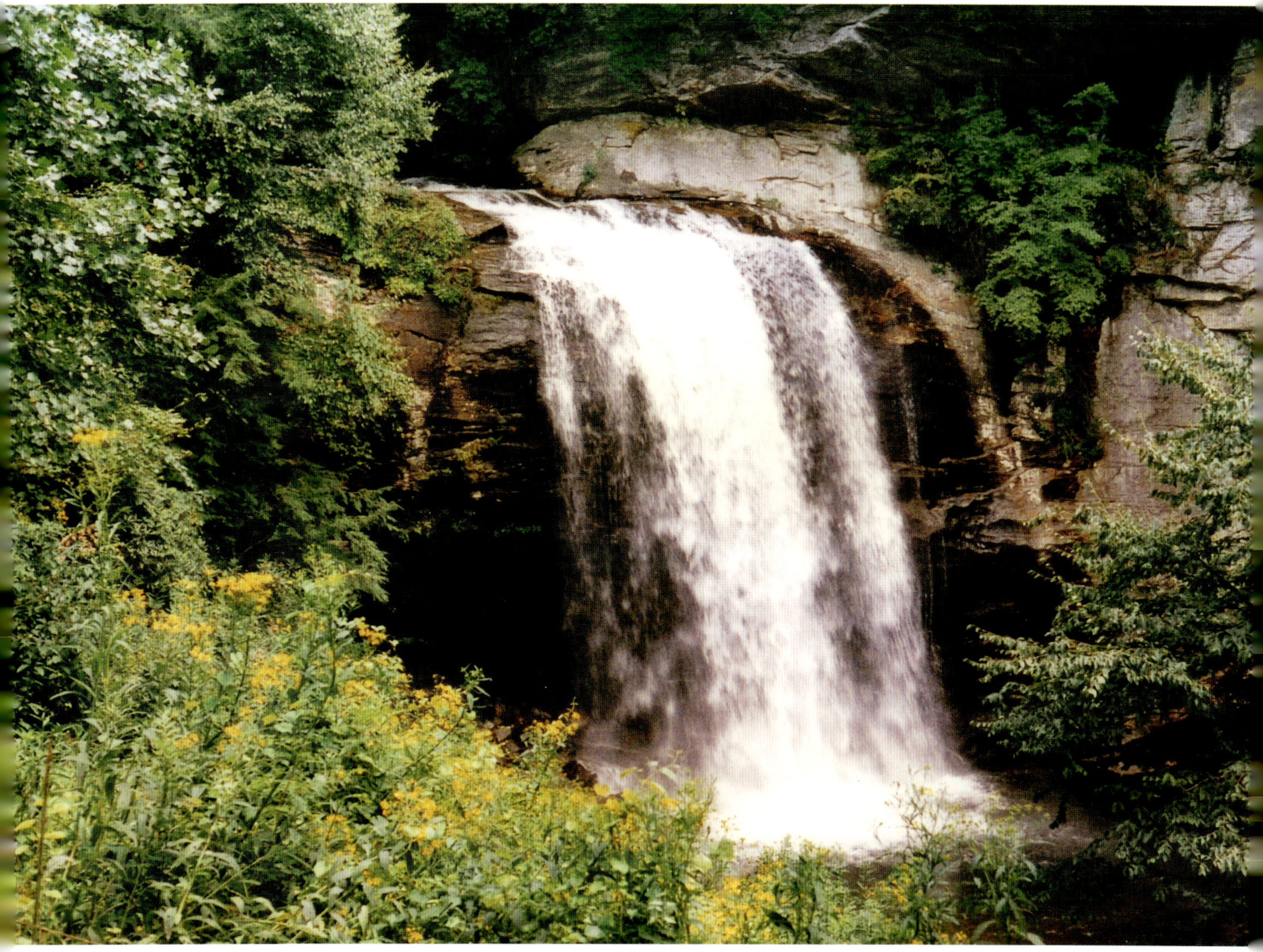

OF THE FOUNTAIN OF THE WATER OF LIFE FREELY

Looking unto **Jesus** the author
and finisher of *our* faith; ...
Hebrews 12 : 2

LORD JESUS CHRIST   ALPHA AND OMEGA   SAVIOR OF THE WORLD   KING OF KINGS   MESSIAH

THE DOOR   THE WAY, THE TRUTH AND THE LIFE   THE WORD OF GOD   BRIGHT AND MORNING STAR

LIGHT OF THE WORLD   PRINCE OF PEACE   IMMANUEL   CHIEF SHEPHERD   THE MIGHTY GOD

PRINCE OF LIFE   APOSTLE AND HIGH PRIEST   ROCK   THE GOOD SHEPHERD   KING OF ISRAEL

THE FIRST BEGOTTEN OF THE DEAD   BREAD OF LIFE   MEDIATOR   LAMB OF GOD   THE CHRIST

ONLY BEGOTTEN SON   ANOINTED   SEED OF DAVID   THE PRINCE OF THE KINGS OF THE EARTH

THE TRUE LIGHT   KING ETERNAL, IMMORTAL, INVISIBLE   HEIR OF ALL THINGS   *LORD OF* GLORY

RABBI   FOUNDATION   CHIEF CORNER *STONE*   THE HOLY ONE OF GOD   MASTER   TEACHER

POTENTATE   LORD OF LORDS   THE EVERLASTING FATHER   THE ROOT AND THE OFFSPRING OF DAVID

GLORIFIED   SON OF MAN   FAITHFUL AND TRUE   THE ONLY WISE GOD   SON OF THE BLESSED

WONDERFUL   COUNSELLOR   THE FAITHFUL WITNESS   BELOVED SON   PERFECT   AUTHOR

THE ALMIGHTY   SON OF THE LIVING GOD   THE BEGINNING AND THE END   SAVIOR JESUS CHRIST

And being made perfect, he became the author of eternal salvation unto all them that obey him;
Hebrews 5 : 9

the photographer

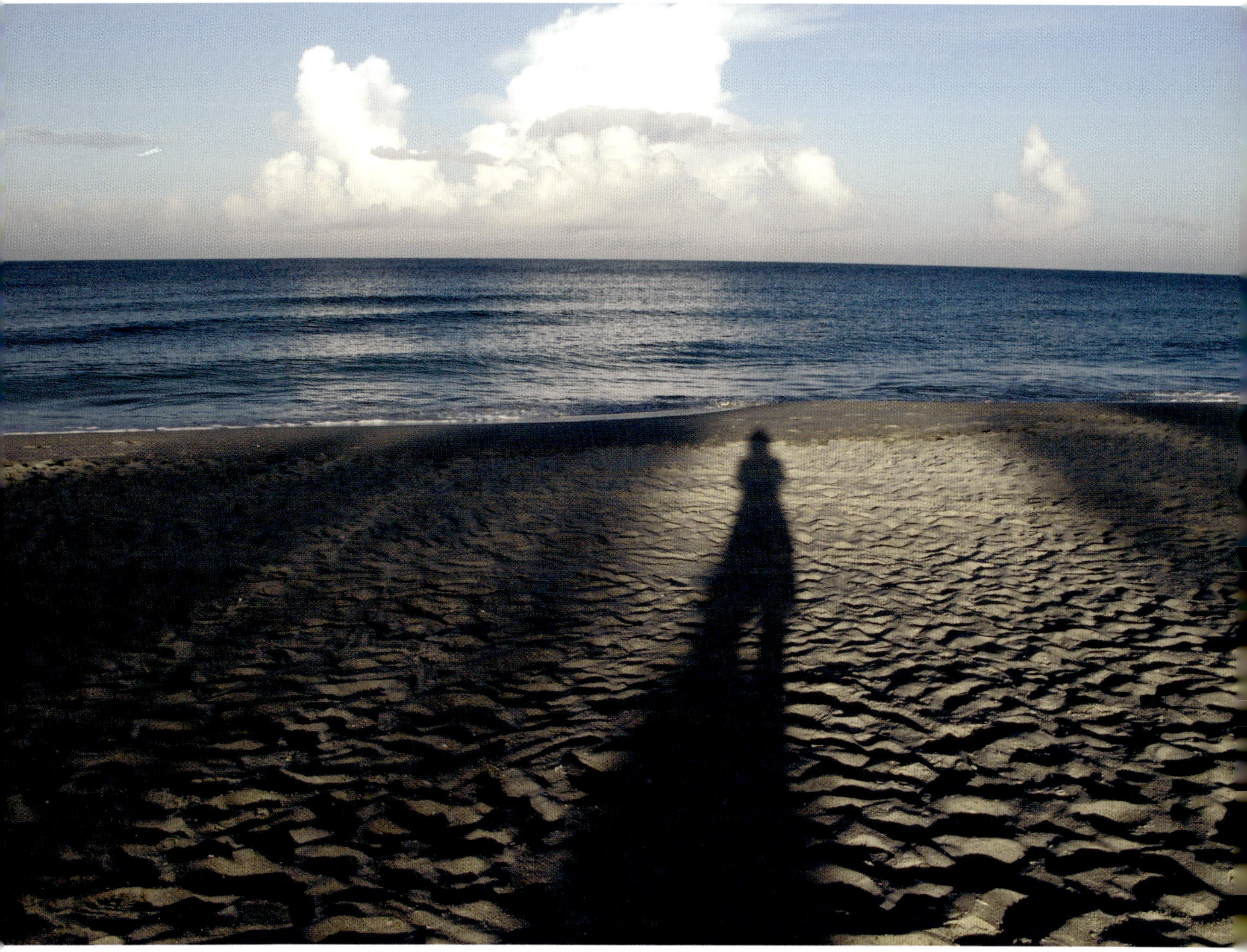

at the beach

LOOKING UNTO JESUS -- REFERENCE GUIDE -- KING JAMES BIBLE

ALPHA AND OMEGA	REVELATION 1:8
ANOINTED	ACTS 10:38
APOSTLE AND HIGH PRIEST	HEBREWS 3:1
AUTHOR	HEBREWS 12:2
BELOVED SON	LUKE 9:35
BREAD OF LIFE	JOHN 6:35
BRIGHT AND MORNING STAR	REVELATION 22:16
CHIEF CORNER *STONE*	EPHESIANS 2:20
CHIEF SHEPHERD	1 PETER 5:4
COUNSELLOR	ISAIAH 9:6
FAITHFUL AND TRUE	REVELATION 19:11
FOUNDATION	1 CORINTHIANS 3:11
GLORIFIED	JOHN 17:10
HEIR OF ALL THINGS	HEBREWS 1:2
IMMANUEL	ISAIAH 7:14
KING ETERNAL, IMMORTAL, INVISIBLE	1 TIMOTHY 1:17
KING OF ISRAEL	MARK 15:32
KING OF KINGS	REVELATION 19:16
LAMB OF GOD	JOHN 1:36
LIGHT OF THE WORLD	JOHN 9:5
LORD JESUS CHRIST	TITUS 1:4
LORD OF GLORY	JAMES 2:1
LORD OF LORDS	REVELATION 19:16
MASTER	MATTHEW 23:10
MEDIATOR	1 TIMOTHY 2:5
MESSIAS (MESSIAH)	JOHN 1:41
ONLY BEGOTTEN SON	JOHN 3:16
PERFECT	HEBREWS 5:9
POTENTATE	1 TIMOTHY 6:15
PRINCE OF LIFE	ACTS 3:15
PRINCE OF PEACE	ISAIAH 9:6
RABBI	JOHN 6:25
ROCK	1 CORINTHIANS 10:4
SAVIOR JESUS CHRIST	2 TIMOTHY 1:10
SAVIOR OF THE WORLD	JOHN 4:42
SEED OF DAVID	JOHN 7:42
SON OF THE BLESSED	MARK 14:61
SON OF MAN	MARK 14:62
SON OF THE LIVING GOD	MATTHEW 16:16
TEACHER	JOHN 3:2
THE ALMIGHTY	REVELATION 1:8
THE BEGINNING AND THE END	REVELATION 21:6
THE CHRIST	MATTHEW 16:16
THE DOOR	JOHN 10:9
THE EVERLASTING FATHER	ISAIAH 9:6
THE FAITHFUL WITNESS	REVELATION 1:5
THE FIRST BEGOTTEN OF THE DEAD	REVELATION 1:5
THE GOOD SHEPHERD	JOHN 10:11
THE HOLY ONE OF GOD	MARK 1:24
THE MIGHTY GOD	ISAIAH 9:6
THE ONLY WISE GOD	1 TIMOTHY 1:17
THE PRINCE OF THE KINGS OF THE EARTH	REVELATION 1:5
THE ROOT AND THE OFFSPRING OF DAVID	REVELATION 22:16
THE TRUE LIGHT	JOHN 1:9
THE WAY, THE TRUTH AND THE LIFE	JOHN 14:6
THE WORD OF GOD	REVELATION 19:13
WONDERFUL	ISAIAH 9:6

BIBLIOGRAPHY

"Bible Study Tools." Christianity.com. 18 Apr. 2008. <http://bible.christianity.com>.

Dake's Annotated Reference Bible Authorized or King James Version Text. 4th ed. Lawrenceville, GA: Dake, Inc., 2002.

Holy Bible Authorized King James Version. Red Letter ed. Iowa Falls, IA: World Bible Publishers Printed in England by Eyre and Spottiswoode (Publishers) Limited Her Majesty's Printers, London.

Holy Bible King James Version. Words of Christ in Red ed. Printed in the United States of America: World Bible, Inc., 1989.

"Information -- Bible Versions." Chick Publications. 18 Apr. 2008. 17 Oct. 2005 <http://www.chick.com>.

"King James Bible - No Pronoun Capitalization." Online Evangelism -- a Guide to Web Outreach. 18 Apr. 2008. 14 July 2007 <http://guide.gospelcom.net>.

The Companion Bible The Authorized Version of 1611 (KJV). Enlarged Type ed. Grand Rapids, MI: Kregel Publications, 1999.

The New Strong's Exhaustive Concordance of the Bible. Nelson's Comfort Print ed. Nashville: Thomas Nelson, Inc., 1995.

The Rainbow Study Bible King James Version. 11th ed. El Reno, OK: Rainbow Studies, Inc., 1996.

"Tetragrammaton." Wikipedia, the Free Encyclopedia. 14 Apr. 2008 <http://en.wikipedia.org>.

Word of God King James Version Easy Reading Study Bible. Red Lettered Large Print Special Margin ed. Goodyear, AZ: G.E.M., 2001.

INDEX

A

abased 99
abide 27
abideth 125
abolished 97
abound 99
Abraham 11, 65, 95
abstain 107
abundantly 111
accept 77
acceptable 119
access 97
accounted 89
acknowledge 39
acknowledging 113
acquit 67
Adam 91, 129
adulterous 79
adversaries 67
adversary 33
afflict 29
affliction 63
afraid 13, 33
agree 123
Ahasuerus 33
Ahava, river of, 29
alive 103
Almighty, *inside back cover*
alpha 131, *inside front cover*
Amaziah 27
angel(s) 75, 89
anger 21, 55, 65, 67
anointed 19
answer 69
answered 79
antichrist 125
apostles 97
appear 87
appeared 87
Apphia 113
appointed 69, 119
archangel 103
Archippus 113
armour 17
army 57
arose 81
ashamed 29, 57
ask 117
asleep 81, 103
athirst 131
author 115
awake 81

B

Baal 71
backsliding 55
banquet 33
baptism 101
Bashan 67
battle 17
beast 71
beautiful 41
beauty 25, 55
beginning 1, 41, 131
begotten 85
believe 83, 93, 103, 107, 119
believed 85, 111
believeth 85, 119, 123
beloved 43, 113, 121, 127
Benjamin 61
blameless 121
blessed 53, 95
blessing 95
blinded 93
blood 45, 97, 123
blotting 101
boast 27
bodies 91
bodily 101
body 35, 91, 93, 97, 101
bondmen 33
bondwomen 33
bones 39
book 35, 67, 95
booths 5
born 5, 41, 123
Branch, The, 75
branches 55
brightness 59, 87
broken 97
brook 5, 17
build 41
builders 119
building 97
built 97, 119
burden 67
buried 15, 101
burned 121

C

calm 81
Canaan 11
captivity 59
care(s) 83, 99
careful 99, 111
carest 81
Carmel 67
celebrate 5
celestial 91
chariot 23
charity 127, 129
Chemarims 71
children 3, 11, 37, 127
See also Israel
chosen 109, 119
Christ, 89, 93, 95, 97, 99, 101, 103, 105, 107, 109, 111, 113, 119, 123, 125, 129
See also **Jesus**
See also **Lord**
church 113, 127
circumcision 101
clean 45
cloud(s) 7, 19, 67, 103, 115, 129
comfort 103
command 105
commanded 93
commanding 107
commandment(s) 7, 37, 39, 97
compassion 65
complete 101
condemn 85
condemnation 85, 129
condemned 85, 111
confess 125
confidence 105
confounded 119
conquerors 89
conscience 107
consider 109, 115
consume 71
consumed 35
contemptible 77
content 99
contradiction 115
contrary 101
conversation 121
convince 129
corruption 63, 91
covenant 19, 37
created 1, 107
cried 23, 31, 63

cross 97, 101, 115
crown 49
crowned 109
cry 35
crying 131
curse 95

D
Damascus 59
dance 41, 49
Daniel 53
darkness 1, 35, 53, 59, 85, 87, 93, 129
daughter(s) 27, 57
David 17, 19, 109
day(s) 63, 65, 75, 101
dead 91, 101, 103, 109, 129
death 15, 89, 131
deceit 101
deceivers 125
deeds 85, 125, 129
delighteth 65
deliver 27
deliverance 61
delivered 105
deliveredst 31
delivering 87
denying 129
descend 103
desire 19
desired 79
desolate 47, 49
despair 93
destroy 35
destroyed 33, 47, 93
devil(s) 83, 107
dew 9, 55
die 15, 41
died 103
diligent 121
discern 79
dishonour 91
disobedient 31, 119
dissolved 121
distil 9
distress 89
distressed 93
divided 1
doctrine(s) 9, 107, 125
dream(s) 57
drink 3, 61, 101
drought 73
dust 67
dwell 5, 51, 55, 131
dwelleth 101, 121
dwelt 11
dying 93

E
ear(s) 9, 13
earth 1, 9, 19, 25, 35, 43, 63, 87, 121, 123
earthen 93
Edom 27
Edomites 27
Egypt 3, 5, 11
elders 3
elements 121
Elijah 23
Elisha 23
Elkoshite 67
embrace 41
end 41, 69, 131
ending, *inside front cover*
endure 109
endured 115
enemies 27, 31, 67
enemy 29, 33
enmity 97
Enoch 129
enquired 71
envies 119
Ephraim 55, 61
Esau, 11
  house of, 61
  mount of, 61
Esther 33
eternal 109, 111, 123
everlasting 19, 37, 85
evil 33, 39, 45, 85, 105, 109, 119, 125
execute 129
eyes 35, 39, 45, 49, 75, 87, 131

F
faint 115
fainted 63
faith 69, 81, 87, 95, 101, 105, 107, 113, 115, 117, 123
faithful 95, 105, 109, 111, 131
faithfully 127
famine 51, 89
fasted 29
Father 97, 113, 123, 125
  See also **God**
  See also **Son**
father(s) 11, 21, 23, 51, 53, 65
fatherless 45
fear 19, 25, 37, 39, 73, 129
feared 25, 81
fearful 13, 81
feast(s) 5, 59, 129
feet 67, 87
fellowcitizens 97
fellowhelpers 127
fellowlaborer 113
fellowsoldier 113
fenced 35
field(s) 25, 37, 51, 61
fire 7, 23, 61, 121
fish 63
fishes 71
flesh 35, 47, 51, 57, 97, 101, 125
flood(s) 11, 63
flourished 99
flourisheth 37
flower(s) 37, 43, 67
foolish 111
forbidding 107
foreigners 97
forgiven 101
forgiveness 87
forsake 29, 39, 49
forsaken 93
forseeing 95
foundation 97
fountain 131
freely 55, 131
fruit(s) 51, 55, 77, 83, 109, 129
furious 67

G
gather 41
gave 85, 123
genealogies 111
generation(s) 5, 49, 79
Gentiles 77, 87, 95, 127
Gideon 13

INDEX

Gilead 61
give 13, 17, 25,
  27, 51, 93, 109,
  131
given 41, 53, 117,
  123
glad 25
glorified 105
glorious 93
glory 25, 91, 93,
  109
God 1, 5, 9, 11,
  15, 19, 27, 29,
  35, 39, 41, 51,
  53, 63, 65, 67,
  73, 85, 87, 89,
  93, 95, 97, 99,
  101, 103, 105,
  107, 111, 113,
  115, 117, 119,
  121, 123, 125,
  129, 131
  glory of, 93
  image of, 93
  Lord, 129
  LORD their, 73
  name of, 53
  Son of, 85, 123
  Spirit of, 1
  tabernacle of, 131
  the LORD your, 57
  trump of, 103
  word of, 83, 109
    See also hosts
    See also **LORD**
god(s) 11, 15, 25,
  27, 59, 93
Godhead 101
godliness 121
godly 127
good 1, 29, 39,
  83, 99, 107,
  109, 111, 113
gospel 93, 95, 109
grace 109, 111,
  113, 129
gracious 119
grass 9, 19, 37
great 25, 57, 67,
  77, 81, 113,
  121
greater 123, 127
greatness 9
ground 73, 83
groves 21
grow 19, 55, 119
groweth 97

H
habitation 97
Haggai 73
Haman 33
hand(s) 3, 13, 17,
  27, 29, 31, 45,
  71, 73, 77, 101,
  115
hangeth 95
hate 41, 59
head 49, 63, 101,
  119
heal 41, 55
health 39, 127
hear 9, 45, 75, 83,
  127
heard 99, 109
hearing 113
heart(s) 27, 33,
  39, 41, 47, 49,
  51, 83, 93, 105
heat 121
heathen 25, 51,
  61, 77, 95
heaven(s) 1, 9, 23,
  25, 31, 37, 41,
  53, 71, 79, 87,
  103, 121, 123,
  131
Hebrew 87
heirs 111
hell 63
heretick 111
heritage 65
hid 93
hide 45
holiness 25, 61
holy 61, 63, 97,
  119, 121
holyday 101
Holy Ghost 111,
  123
honest 83, 99
honour 25
hope 103, 111
Horeb 3
horsemen 23, 29
horses 23
hosts,
  The God of, 59
  the LORD of, 75,
  77
house 19, 113,
  119, 125
    See also Israel
    See also Jacob
    See also Joseph
    See also Esau
household 97
hungry 99
husbandman 109
hypocrisies 119
hypocrisy 107
hypocrites 79

I
idols 25, 55
ignorant 103
image
    See **God**
images 59
incense 77
incorruption 91
increase 51
inhabitants 71
inherit 131
inheritance 87
iniquity 9, 65, 75
instructed 99
Isaac 11
Israel, 13, 21,
  23, 55, 57
Israel, *continued*
  children of, 5, 7
  house of, 59
  Rock of, 19
Israelites 5

J
Jacob, 11, 19, 61
  65
  house of, 61
jealous 67
Jerobaum 21
Jerusalem 71
Jesse 19
Jesus 87, 89, 93
  95, 97, 103,
  107, 109, 111,
  113, 115, 119,
  123, 125, 129,
    See also **Chris**
    See also **Lord**
Joash 27
Jonah 63
Jonas 79
Jordan 23
Josedech 73
Joseph,
  house of, 61
Joshua 11, 73, 7
journey 127
journeyed 7, 87
joy 49, 83, 113,
  115, 117, 127
Judah 27, 71
judge 45, 75, 101

judgement(s) 9, 35, 45, 51, 59, 129
just 69, 95, 99
justified 95, 111

K
kill 3, 41
killed 89
kingdom 37
kings(s) 29, 33, 53, 87
knowledge 53, 93

L
labour 73
laboureth 109
lame 77
land 21, 43, 47, 51, 71, 73, 75
languisheth 67
lasciviousness 129
laugh 41
law 31, 39, 95, 97, 111
learn 45
learned 99
Lebanon 27, 55, 67
liar 123
lie 69
lies 107
life 39, 63, 83, 85, 89, 93, 109, 111, 123, 131
light 1, 19, 53, 59, 85, 87, 93
living 91, 119
look 63, 121, 125
looking 115, 121
LORD 3, 5, 7, 9, 11, 13, 15, 17, 19, 21, 25, 37, 39, 45, 47, 49, 57, 59, 61, 63, 67, 69, 71, 73, 75, 77
See also **God**
See also hosts
Lord 87, 89, 93, 97, 99, 103, 105, 109, 113, 117, 119, 121, 129
See also **Christ**
See also **Jesus**
lose 41, 125
lost 93
love 41, 43, 55, 89, 105, 113
loved 85, 89
lovely 99

M
Malcham 71
malice 119
man 19, 37, 39, 47, 71, 75, 81, 91, 95, 97, 101, 111, 117
manifest 85, 93
mantle 23
marry 107
Master 81
meat(s) 77, 101, 107
melt 121
mercies 31
mercy 37, 39, 65, 111
message 73
messenger 73
Midianites 13
minds 93, 115
minister 87, 107
moon 91, 101
Moses 3
mountain(s) 49, 61, 63, 73
Mount Gilead 13
Mount Seir 11
Mount Zion 61
mourn 41
mourneth 47
mourning 49
mouth 9, 33
multiplied 11
multiply 51
murmured 3

N
Nachor 11
Nahum 67
nailing 101
name(s) 53, 57, 59, 71, 77, 85, 127
nations 25, 95
neighbour 75
newborn 119
night(s) 53, 63, 121
Nineveh 67
nourished 107

O
obey 81
obeyed 73
offence 119
offered 77
offering(s) 25, 59, 77
omega 131, *inside front cover*
opportunity 99
oppressed 45
ordained 129
ordinances 97, 101
overcometh 123, 131

P
pain 131
palace 33
parable 83
pardoneth 65
partition 97
pastors 47
paths 35, 39
patience 83, 115, 117
patient 105
Paul 113
peace 39, 41, 47, 59, 81, 97, 99,
peace *continued* 113, 121
people 3, 11, 13, 15, 25, 33, 51, 57, 73, 87, 131
perfect 9, 117
perfection 83
peril 89
perish 33, 81, 85
perplexed 93
persecuted 93
persecutest 87
persecution 89
persuaded 89
Pharisees 79
Philemon 113
Philistine(s) 17, 61
philosophy 101
plant 41
plead 45
pleasures 83
polluted 77
possess 11, 61
power(s) 29, 67, 87, 89, 91, 93, 101
praise 53, 57, 99
praised 25
pray 105
prayed 63
prayer(s) 45, 63, 107, 113
preach 93
preached 95, 97
precious 119
priest(s) 71, 73

priesthood 119
principalities 89, 101
principality 101
prisoner 113
proclaim 13
proclaimed 29
profaned 77
profit 41
profitable 111
promise 95, 121
prophesied 129
prophesy 57
prophet(s) 31, 73, 79, 97
prosper 127
protested 75
provocations 31
provoking 21
psalmist 19
publish 9
pure 77, 99
purpose 41, 87

Q
queen 33
questions 111
quickened 101
quickening 91

R
race 115
rain 9, 19, 43
raised 91, 101, 109
readeth 69
reason 45, 63
rebelled 31
rebuked 81
rebuketh 67
receive 83, 87, 95, 117, 123, 125, 127
received 99, 107
reconcile 97
record 123
redeemed 95
redeemer 35
refreshed 113
regeneration 111
reject 111
rejected 49
rejoice 5, 25
rejoiced 99, 127
remember 37, 109
remembered 63
remembrance 107
remnant 65, 71, 73
renew 49
renewing 111
reproved 69, 85
respect 101
rested 7
restore 57
resurrection 91
revengeth 67
revive 55
reward 125
riches 83
right 9, 29
righteousness 37, 59, 111, 121
rise 87, 103
risen 101
river(s) 3, 21, 29, 67
Rock, He is the, 9
See also Israel
rock 3, 35, 83, 119
root(s) 21, 55, 83, 129
run 69, 115
Ruth 15

S
sabbath 101
sacrifices 59, 119
Sadducees 79
saints 97, 113, 129
salvation 19, 25, 109
Samaria 61
sanctified 87, 107
Satan 87
Saul 17, 87
save 51
saved 13, 31, 83, 85, 111
saveth 17
Savior, Jesus Christ our, 111
saviours 31
scatter 21
scripture 95, 119
sea(s) 25, 63, 65, 67, 71, 81, 117, 129
season(s) 41, 53
secret 53
seducing 107
seed 11, 83, 109
seek 29, 45
seeketh 79
send 87
separate 89
servant(s) 57, 75, 93
shadow 55, 101, *book cover*
shame 115, 129
Shealtiel 73
sheep 89
shine 93
ship 81
sick 77
sight 63
silence 41
sin(s) 21, 45, 65, 87, 101, 115
sincere 119
sing 25
singing 43
sinned 49
sinners 115, 129
sinneth 111
Sion 119
slain 33, 97
slaughter 89
sleep 103
smell 43, 55, 59
soldier(s) 29, 109
Son, 85, 123, **Father** and the, 125
See also **God**
son(s) 27, 39, 41, 57, 109, 131
songs 59
sorrow 103, 131
soul 63, 69, 91, 127
speak 9, 41, 69, 9
speaking(s) 87, 107, 119
Spirit, 19, 95, 97, 107, 123
See also **God**
spirit(s) 51, 57, 91 107, 123
spiritual 91, 119
stand 35, 75, 87
star(s) 59, 91, 129
statute(s) 5, 51
stone(s) 3, 17, 41, 75, 97, 119
storm 67, 81
strangers 97, 127
stream 59
strength 25
strengtheneth 99
strong 109
stumble 119
stumblingblocks 7
subdue 65

'fer 99, 109
ı 19, 77, 87, 91
ear 71
ord 17, 47, 89
orn 65

ɔernacle 7, 59,
.31, *book cover*
'ry 69
ɜted 119
ıch 109
ırs 131
nple 63, 97
nptation(s) 83,
.17
npting 79
ıt(s) 7
rah 11
restrial 91
ɜtified 31, 123,
.27
ɜtimony 7
ank 53, 113
anksgiving 107
ef 121
nk 99, 117
rst 3

thistle 27
thorns 83
throne 37, 49, 115,131
time(s) 11, 31, 41, 53, 69, 79
Timothy 113
together 97
touching 105
tower 69
tradition 101
transgresseth 125
transgression 65
travail 41
treasure 93
tree(s) 5, 43, 51, 55, 75, 95, 129
trespasses 101
tribulation 89
triumphing 101
trouble 31, 109
troubled 93
true 99, 131
trump 103
trust 39
truth 9, 39, 65, 85, 107, 123, 127

U
uncircumcision 101
understanding 39, 53, 109
ungodly 129
unprofitable 111
unreasonable 105
unstable 117

V
vain 101, 111
vengeance 67
vessels 93
vexed 31
victory 123
vine(s) 43, 55, 75
vineyard 47
virtue 99
vision(s) 53, 57, 67, 69
voice 43, 63, 73, 87, 103, 131
void 1

W
wait 69
waiting 105
walk 49, 51, 75, 127
war 41
wash 45
washing 111
watch 69
water(s) 1, 3, 13, 21, 59, 63, 123, 129, 131
wave(s) 63, 81, 117, 129
wavering 117
weakness 91
wearied 115
weariness 77
weather 79
weep 41
whirlwind 23, 67
wicked 33, 37, 67, 71, 79, 105
widow 45
wife 27
wilderness 47, 59
wind(s) 37, 81, 117, 129
wine 33, 55, 73
wisdom 53, 117
wise 39, 53
witness 37, 87, 109, 123, 127
witnesses 109, 115
Word 123
word(s) 9, 19, 33, 35, 73, 83, 101, 103, 105, 107, 109, 119, 131
work(s) 9, 25, 41, 95, 111, 117, 121
world 25, 41, 85, 93, 101, 123, 125
worship 25, 71
wrath 29, 33, 67, 71
write 39, 69, 131
written 35, 89, 91, 95
wrong 35

Z
Zerubbabel
Zion,
mountain of, 49

Note: This Index can be used for a deeper study of God's Word. For example, using a concordance you will see that the word Zion (translated from Hebrew) is used in the Old Testament. It is the same word Sion (translated from Greek) that is used in the New Testament. The concordance will reveal that both words mean a mountain or hill of Jerusalem. You can also see how some words may have a different meaning depending on the context in which they are used.

Please also see Page iii -- Looking Unto Jesus Reference Guide for further study in the King James Bible.